# FAITH, FAVOR, AND FUNDING

How One Mother's Determination Turned Scholarships into Generational Blessings.

ABBIE P. HUCKLEBY

# COPYRIGHT

**Title:** Faith, Favor, and Funding

**Subtitle:** How One Mother's Determination Turned Scholarships into Generational Blessings.

**Author:** Abbie P. Huckleby



Parent Project LLC

Scholarship Preparation Program

Email: abbie@parentprojectllc.com

Phone: 832-600-5413

Website: www.parentprojectllc.com

Scripture quotations are used for educational and inspirational purposes. All personal stories are based on true experiences shared with permission.

Printed in the United States of America

# DEDICATION

For my daughters, Alayna and Laura, whose faith, hard work, and determination inspired every page of this book.

For every parent who dares to dream bigger for their children.

For every student who refuses to give up, no matter how difficult the journey may feel.

And for every family walking by faith, trusting Yahuah to provide, may this book remind you that preparation and prayer can open doors no one can close.

***

# ACKNOWLEDGMENTS

I would like to acknowledge my daughters, whose journeys inspired the birth of this work.

To my family, for their unwavering support, and to every family I've had the privilege to help. Your faith and persistence continue to motivate me.

A special thank you to Barbara, whose encouragement and inspired dream helped bring this book to life.

To my beta readers, thank you for taking the time to read this manuscript before it reached the world. Your honest feedback, thoughtful insights, and encouragement strengthened every page. This book is better because of you.

And to Yahuah, who turned a mother's worry into wisdom and a personal struggle into a ministry that blesses others. All glory belongs to You.

***

# TABLE OF CONTENTS

# FOREWORD

*By Barbara Payne-Jenkins*

I'll never forget the conversation that started it all.

Abbie and I were talking one evening, and she shared her story with me. How she'd had to leave Tuskegee Institute years ago because she couldn't find the funding to stay. How that loss had shaped her. How she was determined her daughters would have a different story.

But what struck me most wasn't just her determination. It was her faith. Abbie didn't just want her daughters to go to college. She wanted them to go debt-free, and she believed God would make a way.

I watched her pray over scholarship applications. I watched her organize binders and spreadsheets late into the night. I watched her encourage her daughters through rejections and celebrate with them when award letters arrived. And I watched God honor her faithfulness in ways that left us all in awe.

When both Alayna and Laura graduated debt-free with over $450,000 in scholarships combined, I knew this story couldn't stay quiet. This wasn't just about one family's success. This was a blueprint. A roadmap. A testimony that needed to be shared.

I encouraged Abbie to write this book because I've seen firsthand the impact of her work. I've watched families overwhelmed by college costs find hope again. I've seen students who doubted themselves discover confidence. I've witnessed parents who felt helpless learn that they could take control of their children's futures.

Abbie's guidance also inspired my own journey. When my goddaughter, Sani, graduated high school in 2020, I had the same desire to help her pursue college debt-free. I followed the model that was laid out for me, and it worked. That's the power of what Abbie teaches. It's replicable, practical, and rooted in faith.

What you're holding in your hands isn't just a book about scholarships. It's a book about faith in action. It's about what happens when you combine prayer with preparation, belief with strategy, and trust with hard work.

Abbie doesn't just tell you what to do. She shows you. She walks you through every step, from the first scholarship search to the final award letter. She shares her mistakes, her victories, her fears, and her breakthroughs. And most importantly, she reminds you that God is faithful, even when the path ahead feels impossible.

If you're a parent standing at the kitchen table surrounded by college brochures and financial aid forms, unsure of how you'll make it work, this book is for you.

If you're a student who dreams of going to college but can't yet see a way forward, this book is for you.

If you're a family that believes in the power of faith but needs practical steps to walk it out, this book is for you.

Abbie's story is proof that where you start doesn't determine where you finish. That debt doesn't have to be inevitable. That with God, preparation, and persistence, doors will open that no one can close.

I'm honored to introduce you to a woman whose faith changed her family's trajectory and whose mission is now changing countless others. Read this book. Apply what you learn. Trust the process. And watch God turn your faith into provision.

*Barbara Payne-Jenkins*

***

# PREFACE

Let me share with you why I'm so passionate about this book.

I went to Tuskegee Institute back in 1980, full of hope and determination. Unfortunately, I had to leave school because I lacked the knowledge or support from my family or the school administrators to find funding that could have helped me stay. That experience stayed with me for years. It shaped me. And when I became a mother to my two daughters, I was determined they would not face the same fate.

My husband and I knew that, on our salaries, we couldn't afford college for two daughters who would be in school at the same time. So I started early, researching ways to find money to send them and keep them in school. I prayed. I organized. I applied. And we did just that.

Both of my daughters graduated debt-free with over $450,000 in scholarships combined. But this book isn't just about what we accomplished. It's about what you can accomplish too.

Now, I want to share what we've learned and experienced so that other families can do the same. If you're a parent who feels overwhelmed by college costs, a student who doubts whether higher education is possible, or a family standing at the starting line unsure of where to begin, this book is for you.

What began as a personal journey has become my life's work, and I'm honored to walk this path with you.

***

# AUTHOR'S NOTE ON FAITH

Throughout this book, you'll see me use the name Yahuah when speaking of the Father. I now use His original Hebrew name because that's how I've come to know Him personally. It reminds me that my faith isn't based on tradition or titles, but on a living relationship with the One who has guided, provided, and restored every part of my life.

The lessons in this book come from real experiences, from searching for scholarships late into the night to celebrating each award letter that arrived in the mail. I want you to know that it's possible to send your children to college without debt, with faith as your foundation and preparation as your plan.

If my story can give you hope, then every obstacle I faced was worth it. My prayer is that this book will help your family discover the same peace, joy, and favor we experienced, and remind you that with Yahuah, nothing is impossible.

***

# PART I: THE JOURNEY BEGINS

# CHAPTER 1: THE JOURNEY BEGINS

*A Mother's Faith and Determination*

The house was quiet that night. Everyone had gone to bed, and the only sound was the hum of the refrigerator and the sigh of the Texas wind against the kitchen window. I sat at the table, surrounded by stacks of college brochures, printouts, and bills. My coffee had gone cold, but I did not notice. My mind was racing faster than my heart.

Alayna and Laura were still in high school, bright and ambitious, already talking about their college dreams as if they were right around the corner. They made me proud. They had worked hard and carried themselves with the kind of grace that makes a mother's heart swell. But as I flipped through tuition numbers and cost-of-living estimates, reality hit me. We couldn't afford it.

My husband and I had steady jobs, but between the mortgage, bills, and everyday expenses, there wasn't enough left to cover two college educations at the same time. I did the math over and over, hoping the numbers would somehow change. They never did. Each time I added up our income and subtracted our obligations, the gap remained. Wide. Unmovable. Impossible.

I thought about my own story. Years ago, I walked the hills and valleys of Tuskegee Institute with big dreams, but without the right guidance or resources to find funding, I had to leave before finishing. The weight of that decision never left me. The shame I felt walking away from campus. The look on my mother's face when I told her I couldn't stay. The unfinished degree that haunted me for years.

"I started at Tuskegee," I would say, and then I'd change the subject before they could ask why I didn't finish.

I carried that disappointment for so long. It sat heavy in my chest every time someone asked where I went to college. That pain was something I never wanted my daughters to experience.

I promised myself then that my children would never face that heartbreak. They wouldn't have to choose between their dreams and our budget. They wouldn't have to leave school halfway through because the money ran out. They would finish what they started, and they would do it without drowning in debt.

I stared at the papers spread across the table, each one a reminder of both the dream and the obstacle. **Tuition** costs. Room and board. Meal plans. Books. Lab fees. Technology fees. Student activities fees. The list went on. And both girls would be in school at the same time. The numbers were staggering.

According to the College Board, the average annual cost for a student attending a four-year public university in-state is $11,600, and for private universities, it's $45,000. For two daughters attending at the same time, we were looking at around $93,000 over four years if both attended public universities. I knew what the alternative looked like. The average college graduate with student loans left school owing nearly $40,000. Sixty percent of students were graduating with debt. I had read the reports about young people delaying homeownership, putting off starting families, and struggling to save for retirement because of student loan payments. That wasn't going to be my daughters' story.

The question wasn't whether my girls would go to college. It was how.

I whispered a quiet prayer, "Yahuah, show me the way." In that still moment, determination rose in me. Not hope. Not optimism. Determination. If there was a path to a debt-free education, I was going to find it. I didn't care how long it took or how hard I had to work. My daughters were going to college, and they were going to finish.

The next morning, I began. I searched online for scholarships, printed everything that looked promising, and started building a system that could hold the weight of what we were about to do. I didn't have all the answers yet, but I knew I needed a way to stay organized and intentional.

The internet felt like a maze at first. Hundreds of scholarship websites. Thousands of opportunities. Some required essays. Some required videos. Some asked for recommendations. Some wanted transcripts. Some had deadlines in a few weeks. Others had deadlines months away. I didn't know where to start, so I started everywhere.

I bookmarked websites. I signed up for email alerts. I printed applications and eligibility requirements and spread them across the kitchen table. My husband walked through and asked what I was doing. I told him I was building our future. He nodded and went to make more coffee.

I called guidance counselors, asked questions at PTA meetings, and even visited the library for resources most people overlooked. One librarian at our local branch showed me a reference book that listed local scholarships. She said it had been sitting on the shelf for months and no one ever checked it out. I took it home and copied every scholarship my daughters might qualify for.

I learned quickly that scholarships were everywhere. Churches offered them. Civic organizations offered them. Businesses offered them. Alumni groups offered them. Some were for specific majors. Some were for students with certain GPAs. Some were for kids who played sports or participated in band or volunteered in their communities. The opportunities were endless if you knew where to look.

Every evening after work and dinner, I returned to what I had gathered. The girls would laugh and say, "Mama's doing her scholarship homework," and I would smile because that's exactly what it felt like. At first, the process overwhelmed me, but slowly I began to see patterns. Some scholarships valued leadership. Others focused on service or creativity. There was something for everyone, including my daughters.

I started taking notes in a spiral notebook. Which scholarships required essays. Which ones needed recommendation letters. Which deadlines were approaching first. Which ones asked for financial information. Which ones were renewable? Which ones were one-time awards. I wrote it all down.

Then I bought a three-ring binder and organized everything properly. I created sections for applications, essays, deadlines, transcripts, recommendation letters, and financial documents. I used dividers and sheet protectors. I color-coded deadlines on a calendar that I taped to the inside cover. That binder became my command center. My war room. My roadmap to paying for college.

My husband would come home from work and find me at the kitchen table surrounded by papers. He would shake his head and ask if I was going to bed anytime soon. I told him I would sleep when the scholarships were submitted. He never complained. He knew what this meant to me. He knew what it meant for our daughters.

Sometimes late at night, when I was alone at that table, exhaustion would set in. My eyes would blur from reading eligibility requirements. My hand would cramp from writing notes. I would look at the clock and realize it was past midnight. Again. Part of me wanted to close the binder and go to bed. But then I would think about Alayna sitting in her first college class. I would picture Laura walking across a graduation stage. I would remember my own unfinished journey at Tuskegee and how I swore my daughters would have what I didn't.

That vision kept me going. It pushed me through the late nights and the moments of doubt. It reminded me why this mattered.

The more I learned, the more confident I became. I realized this wasn't about luck, connections, or having a child who was valedictorian. This was about consistency. Persistence. Organization. And faith.

I began guiding Alayna and Laura as they worked on their essays, encouraging them to let their light shine. I told them, "Your story matters. Don't be afraid to tell me."

Alayna resisted at first. Writing about herself felt uncomfortable. She didn't want to sound like she was bragging. I told her there was a difference between bragging and being honest about who you are and what you've accomplished. Scholarship committees wanted to know her, not just her GPA.

Laura struggled too, but for different reasons. She was quieter than her sister, more reserved. She said she didn't know what made her special. I sat beside her at the table and asked her questions. What motivates you? What do you care about? What kind of person do you want to become?

Her answers became the foundation for her essays.

We spent hours talking through their experiences. The leadership roles they had taken. The community service they had done. The challenges they had overcome. The dreams they carried. Those conversations were some of the most meaningful moments of my life. I wasn't just helping them write essays. I was helping them see themselves clearly.

I watched my daughters grow through this process. They became more confident, more articulate, more aware of their own strengths. The scholarship search was teaching them skills they would carry for life. How to present themselves. How to meet deadlines. How to handle rejection. How to celebrate success with humility and gratitude.

Then one day it happened. A letter came in the mail addressed to Alayna. Her first scholarship. I'll never forget the sound of her laughter or the tears that followed. It wasn't just joy. It was relief, validation, and hope. That first award sent adrenaline through us, and we were hooked.

The scholarship was $500. Not a fortune, but it was proof. Proof that the process worked. Proof that someone saw value in my daughter. Proof that all those late nights were worth it. I taped that letter to the refrigerator where I could see it every morning. Laura watched her sister celebrate and something shifted in her. She stopped asking if scholarships were real and started asking how many more they could apply for. We had momentum now.

Soon after, I learned a powerful lesson about being in the right place at the right time. One afternoon in the employee cafeteria, I overheard coworkers talking about a dependent scholarship program my company offered. I had worked there for years and never knew it existed. I thanked Yahuah quietly for placing me in that moment.

I didn't finish my lunch. I went straight to Human Resources and asked about the program. The woman behind the desk seemed surprised. She told me most employees didn't know about it. I asked why. She said that once a year they posted it on the company's website and sent an email, but most people probably deleted it without reading.

She sent me the link to the online application. I read every word on my lunch break. The scholarship was for dependents of employees who demonstrated academic achievement and leadership. Alayna qualified because she was a senior that year, and Laura would become eligible the following year. That evening, Alayna and I sat at the computer and completed each section carefully.

That year, Alayna received the $16,000 company dependent scholarship. When Laura's turn came, she was named as an alternate. I explained to her what that meant. If one of the primary recipients didn't meet the requirements or forfeited the scholarship, she would be next in line. She nodded, but I could see the disappointment in her eyes. Being an alternate felt like almost winning but not quite.

Then Yahuah showed up in His perfect timing. One of the scholarship recipients didn't maintain the required GPA and forfeited the remaining balance of his award. He had already used $4,000 during his first year, which left $12,000 available. Laura received that $12,000. What started as disappointment turned into provision. It reminded me once again how Yahuah always places you where you need to be, even when the path looks different than you expected.

Those company scholarships changed everything. They covered significant portions of tuition and gave us room to breathe. More importantly, they gave my daughters confidence. They stopped wondering if they were good enough and started believing they were worthy. And Laura learned a lesson that would serve her well. Sometimes being the alternate is exactly where you need to be. Sometimes waiting is part of the blessing.

From that moment on, I knew we were on the right path. More letters came. More blessings followed. What began as a desperate collection of papers slowly became proof that faith and effort were working together.

It wasn't easy. There were rejections and moments of doubt, but every no made the yeses sweeter. Faith kept me steady. Some applications disappeared into silence. Some essays went unanswered. But I kept a folder of every acceptance letter, every award notification, every check that arrived in the mail. When doubt tried to creep in, I pulled out that folder and remembered what Yahuah was doing.

Looking back, that night at the kitchen table wasn't a breaking point. It was the beginning. It was the night faith met action and a mother's mission was born. I didn't know then that this journey would change our family forever. I didn't know it would become my calling. I didn't know that one day I would sit across from other worried parents and tell them the same thing I'm telling you now.

It's possible. It takes work. It takes faith. It takes organization and persistence. But it's absolutely possible to send your children to college without debt. I'm living proof. My daughters are living proof. And if Yahuah did it for us, He can do it for you.

### *From the Author's Voice:*

*"When I started this journey, I didn't have a roadmap, just faith, determination, and a binder full of possibilities. That was all it took to begin."*

***

# CHAPTER 2: RIGHT ON TIME

———————— ♦ ————————

*Trusting Yahuah's Timing in Every Opportunity*

After the scholarships started rolling in, something inside me shifted. The fear that once sat heavy in my stomach faded away. In its place came faith, confidence, and a sense of calm. What once felt impossible now felt achievable.

I realized scholarships weren't about luck. They were the result of preparation, consistency, and faith working together. Once I started paying attention, I noticed a rhythm to how opportunities appeared. Some came through research and effort. Others came through conversations and connections. And some came purely through divine timing, like the afternoon I overheard a conversation that later led to both of my daughters receiving a company scholarship.

That moment taught me to listen more closely. Yahuah doesn't always answer prayers with dramatic signs. Sometimes he answers through a quiet nudge, a shared table, or a conversation you were never meant to join but were meant to hear. I learned to pay attention to everything. A flyer on a bulletin board. An announcement at church. A casual mention in the break room. Every conversation became an opportunity. Every interaction held potential.

I started carrying a small notebook everywhere I went. When someone mentioned a scholarship program, I wrote it down. When I saw a poster advertising financial aid workshops, I noted the date and time. When a coworker talked about their child receiving an award, I asked questions. Where did they apply? What were the requirements? When was the deadline? People were often surprised by my interest, but I didn't care. My daughters' futures were more important than looking nosy.

That notebook became as essential as my binder at home. I kept it in my purse so it was always within reach. During lunch breaks, I'd flip through the pages and transfer information into our main tracking system. Some entries were just names of organizations. Others were full details about scholarship amounts and deadlines. Every piece of information mattered because I never knew which opportunity would open the next door.

As the results began to show, people started asking questions. Friends, coworkers, and church members wanted to know how we were finding scholarships. At first, I shared small tips in passing. But I quickly realized these questions came from anxiety, not curiosity. Parents were overwhelmed and unsure where to start, just like I had been.

One Sunday after church, a mother approached me in the parking lot. Her daughter was a junior in high school with good grades and big dreams. She asked if I had a few minutes to talk. We stood beside my car for nearly an hour while I explained the basics. Where to search. How to organize. What to focus on first. She took notes on the back of her church bulletin. Before leaving, she hugged me and said, "I didn't know where to start. Thank you for showing me it's possible."

That conversation stayed with me. I realized how many families were stuck in the same place I had been that night at my kitchen table. Worried. Overwhelmed. Unsure. They needed someone to tell them it could be done and to show them how to begin.

That's when I understood this journey was bigger than my household. I began sitting with other parents, walking them through the basics. How to search. How to prepare. How to help their children tell their stories honestly. I watched fear turn into focus. I watched panic turn into purpose. And I came to understand that scholarships aren't reserved for a select few. They're available to anyone willing to show up and stay committed.

I started inviting parents to my house for informal workshops. We'd sit around my dining room table with laptops and printouts spread everywhere. I showed them the websites I used. I walked them through my binder system. I explained how to break down the process into manageable steps so it didn't feel so overwhelming. Some parents came alone. Some brought their teenagers. Some brought notepads and asked questions for an hour straight.

The first workshop I hosted had three families. By the third workshop, I had twelve families crowded into my living room. Word was spreading. Parents were telling other parents. Students were telling their friends. What started as informal help was becoming something bigger. I didn't have a business plan or a formal program yet. I just had a kitchen table, a binder full of information, and a willingness to share what I had learned.

Every session reinforced what I already knew. Information wasn't the problem. Belief was the problem. Most parents didn't think scholarships were for their kids. They assumed scholarships were only for valedictorians or athletes or students from well-resourced schools. I told them that was a myth. Scholarships exist for all kinds of students. You just have to know where to look and be willing to apply.

I also noticed another pattern. Many parents were afraid to ask for help because they thought they should already know how to do this. They felt embarrassed admitting they didn't understand financial aid forms or scholarship applications. I told them there was no shame in not knowing. I didn't know either when I started. Nobody teaches you this in school. You learn by doing, and you do better when someone who has already walked the path shows you the way.

Research shows that most students begin their scholarship search during their junior year of high school, with application deadlines peaking between January and March of senior year. Typically, scholarship notification periods range from one to three months after the deadline, though larger national programs may take four to six months to announce winners. Understanding this timeline helps families plan their search strategically and avoid the last-minute panic that causes many students to miss opportunities.

Around that same time, I stared at a scholarship deadline calendar for the first time and nearly shut my laptop. Deadlines filled the screen. Juniors. Seniors. Incoming freshmen. Even middle school students. Where do you even begin?

What I learned is this. There's no perfect starting point. There's only the decision to begin.

Scholarships aren't just for seniors scrambling at the last minute. There are opportunities for students as young as thirteen, based on leadership, service, creativity, and character. The earlier you start, the more prepared and confident you become. And if you start late, that doesn't disqualify you.

We treated scholarship preparation like a long-term commitment, not a last-minute task. While others waited until senior year, we were already learning the process, strengthening writing skills, and gathering materials. That head start removed pressure. We weren't rushing. We were ready.

The day Alayna brought home a flyer for a local leadership scholarship, she hesitated. She thought she was too early. I told her the earlier you begin; the more doors you open. She applied and later received her first local award. The amount was modest, but the lesson was powerful. The process works when you work it.

That scholarship was only $250, but it taught Alayna something money couldn't buy. It taught her that she was capable. That her story mattered. That people outside our family saw value in who she was becoming. That small award planted a seed of confidence that grew with every application she completed.

That moment changed everything. Scholarships were no longer just about money. They became about momentum. Every application builds confidence. Every essay sharpened clarity. Every rejection strengthened resolve.

Laura learned from watching her sister. By the time she reached her senior year, she was organized, focused, and confident. She once told me it felt like a job, but one that paid for her dreams. She was right.

I told both of my daughters that applying for scholarships was their part-time job during high school. Yes, they both also had actual jobs, but their primary focus was scholarships. The math made sense: spending 10 hours on a scholarship application that paid $2,000 meant earning $200 per hour. No entry-level job could compete with that return. A few hours spent writing an essay could result in a $5,000 award. Show me a part-time job that pays that well.

They didn't always see it that way. There were evenings when they were tired. Times when they wanted to hang out with friends instead of writing another essay. Moments when they complained about deadlines and requirements. I understood their frustration, but I didn't let them quit. I reminded them why this mattered. I reminded them of my unfinished degree from Tuskegee. I reminded them that the work they were doing now would give them freedom later.

Sometimes I had to be firm. When Alayna wanted to skip an application because the essay prompt seemed too hard, I sat beside her and helped her break it down. When Laura complained about writing yet another personal statement, I reminded her that every word she wrote was an investment in her future. I wasn't trying to be harsh. I was trying to teach them that discipline and delayed gratification separate dreams from reality.

I also saw this truth play out with students who started late. One young woman began applying near the end of her senior year, convinced she had missed her chance. I told her she was right on time. Within months, awards began to arrive.

Her name was Jasmine, and she came to me through a referral from her guidance counselor. She was a good student with a solid GPA, but she hadn't applied for a single scholarship. Her family assumed they would take out loans like everyone else. When I asked why she hadn't started sooner, she shrugged and said she didn't think she would win anything.

I looked at her transcript and her list of activities. She had been in student government. She volunteered at a nursing home every weekend. She was part of the debate team. I told her she was exactly the kind of student scholarship committees wanted to support. She didn't believe me at first, but I convinced her to try.

We worked together for three months. She applied for twenty scholarships before graduation. She won four. Those four awards totaled nearly $15,000. When she called to tell me about the last one, she was crying. She said, "Ms. Abbie, I almost gave up. I almost didn't apply for this one because I was tired." I told her that perseverance separates those who receive scholarships from those who don't.

Jasmine taught me something important. She taught me that late starts don't mean lost opportunities. She also taught me that belief is half the battle. Once she started winning, her entire attitude changed. She went from doubting herself to expecting success. That shift in mindset made all the difference. That experience confirmed something I now tell everyone: Opportunity doesn't pass you by. It waits for you to show up.

When parents ask me when to start applying for scholarships, my answer is always the same. Start today. Start where you are. Start with what you have. Whether your child is in middle school, high school, or already in college, there are opportunities waiting.

I've watched students start in ninth grade and build impressive portfolios by graduation. I've also watched students start in the spring of their senior year and still secure enough funding to make college affordable. The key isn't when you start. The key is that you start and that you don't stop.

Timing matters, but faith matters more. I've seen scholarships appear at the last possible moment when families were ready to give up. I've seen awards arrive in the mail weeks after deadlines passed, awarded to students who applied months earlier and had forgotten they even submitted the application. I've seen opportunities open that weren't listed on any website or database, simply because someone paid attention and asked the right question at the right time.

Yahuah's timing isn't our timing. That lesson became clearer with every award letter that arrived. Some scholarships we applied for in the fall weren't awarded until the following summer. Some deadlines we thought we missed turned out to have extensions. Some opportunities we almost skipped ended up being the most significant.

One scholarship Alayna applied for had a deadline in October of her senior year. We submitted everything on time and then heard nothing for months. By March, we had written it off as a rejection. Then in late April, just weeks before graduation, an award letter arrived. She had won. The scholarship was worth $10,000 and renewable for four years if she maintained a certain GPA. That one late notification ended up being one of her largest awards.

Once you see scholarships differently, everything changes. Fear gives way to clarity. Hesitation turns into action. And what once felt out of reach becomes possible, one faithful step at a time.

I learned to trust the process even when results were slow. I learned to celebrate small wins while waiting for bigger ones. I learned that consistency always wins over intensity. It's better to apply for two scholarships a week for six months than to apply for twenty scholarships in one frantic weekend and then burn out.

This journey taught me patience. It taught me persistence. It taught me that faith without works is dead, but works without faith will leave you exhausted. You need both. You need to do the research, fill out the applications, write the essays, and meet the deadlines. But you also need to trust that Yahuah is guiding the process and opening doors you can't see yet.

Looking back, I'm grateful we started when we did. I'm grateful for every scholarship application we submitted early on that taught my daughters how to write about themselves. I'm grateful for every rejection that built resilience. I'm grateful for every late night at the kitchen table that reminded us why we were doing this.

But I'm also grateful for the families who started late and still succeeded. Their stories remind me that it's never too late to begin. Yahuah doesn't operate on our schedules. He operates on purpose and calling. If He has placed college in your child's future, He will make a way. Your job is to show up, do the work, and trust His timing.

### From the Author's Voice:

"*The perfect time to start is now. Yahuah doesn't bless procrastination; He blesses preparation.*"

***

# CHAPTER 3: HIDDEN IN PLAIN SIGHT

*Finding the Blessings Waiting All Around You*

When I first began searching for scholarships, I assumed most opportunities came from colleges or large organizations. I quickly learned that some of the best scholarships are hidden in plain sight.

Every community has resources many families overlook. Local businesses, churches, civic groups, alumni organizations, and employers often offer scholarships that go unclaimed simply because no one asks. Once I realized this, I began looking closer to home.

The shift in my thinking happened one afternoon when I was standing in line at the grocery store. I noticed a flyer taped to the bulletin board near the entrance. It was faded and half covered by other announcements, but I could make out the words "scholarship" and "local students." I pulled out my notebook and wrote down the organization's name and phone number. When I got home, I called and asked for information. The woman who answered seemed surprised. She said they'd been offering the scholarship for five years, but they rarely received more than three or four applications.

That moment opened my eyes. Scholarships were everywhere, but nobody was looking for them.

I started paying attention differently. I looked at bulletin boards in grocery stores, libraries, community centers, and coffee shops. I read church bulletins cover to cover instead of just skimming them. I listened to announcements at PTA meetings instead of letting my mind wander. I asked questions everywhere I went.

I talked to counselors, employers, and community leaders. I paid attention to flyers, bulletin boards, and announcements others ignored. Using the tracking system, we'd built, I added each opportunity to our list and followed up consistently.

School counselors became one of my most valuable resources. I made it a point to visit the guidance office regularly, not just when Alayna and Laura had appointments. I introduced myself to every counselor in the building and asked them to keep my daughters in mind when scholarship information came across their desks. Some counselors were helpful and proactive. Others were overwhelmed and understaffed. I learned quickly which ones to check in with regularly and which ones required more persistence on my part.

One counselor told me something I'll never forget. She said, "Mrs. Huckleby, most parents wait for me to tell them about scholarships. You're the only parent who comes looking."

That comment confirmed what I already suspected. Opportunity favors the persistent.

Employer-based scholarships became especially important. Many companies offer dependent scholarships that employees are unaware of. Asking questions and paying attention made the difference. Those opportunities became some of the most impactful awards my daughters received.

After I discovered my own company's scholarship program, I started asking other parents where they worked. I encouraged them to check with their Human Resources departments. I told them to ask specifically about dependent scholarships, tuition assistance programs, and employee benefits that extended to children. Many parents came back surprised. They'd worked at their companies for years without knowing these programs existed.

One father I spoke with worked for a utility company. He'd been there for fifteen years. When I asked if his employer offered scholarships, he said he didn't think so. I told him to ask anyway. Two weeks later, he called me. His company had a scholarship program that awarded up to $5,000 per year to dependents of employees. He'd never known because the information was buried in an employee handbook he'd never read. His daughter applied and won. He thanked me with a gratitude I could feel.

These stories reinforced something I already believed. Most people miss opportunities not because the opportunities don't exist, but because they don't ask the right questions or look in the right places.

I also learned that local scholarships often have less competition than national ones. A national scholarship might receive thousands of applications. A local scholarship offered by a small business or community organization might receive ten. The odds were significantly better, and the money was just as real.

National scholarships typically receive anywhere from hundreds to tens of thousands of applications, making competition fierce. In contrast, local community scholarships, employer-sponsored programs, and regional awards often receive only a few dozen to fewer than one hundred applicants. Many employer tuition assistance programs, often administered through organizations like Scholarship America, go underutilized simply because employees don't know they exist. These company-sponsored scholarships can range from a few thousand dollars to $5,000 or more per year and represent some of the best opportunities for families willing to ask their Human Resources departments about available programs.

One local scholarship was offered by P.I.E. (Progress In Education), a local nonprofit organization that had been in our community for several years. The application was simple. A one-page form. A short essay about community service. A recommendation letter. The award was $1,000. Alayna applied, and she was one of only six applicants. She won. That scholarship taught me to never overlook opportunities just because they seem small or unfamiliar.

Online scholarship databases also became part of our routine. Sites like Fastweb, Cappex, Scholarships.com, and

Bold.org helped us uncover opportunities we wouldn't have found otherwise. Each day, we checked for new listings and added them to our system. What started as a habit became momentum.

I set up profiles for both of my daughters on multiple scholarship websites. The profiles asked detailed questions about their academic interests, extracurricular activities, community service, and career goals. The more detailed the profile, the better the matches. These sites sent email alerts when new scholarships that fit their profiles became available.

At first, I was skeptical. I assumed the emails would be spam or scams. But I learned to distinguish legitimate opportunities from fake ones. Legitimate scholarships never ask for application fees. They never require you to pay to access information. They never guarantee that you'll win. Once I understood what to look for, the databases became incredibly useful tools.

Every morning, I'd check my email for scholarship alerts. I'd forward relevant opportunities to my daughters and add them to our tracking spreadsheet. We treated it like a job. Consistency mattered more than intensity. A little effort every day produced better results than occasional bursts of activity followed by long periods of inaction.

Over time, we developed a rhythm. Research during the week. Writing and reviewing on evenings or weekends. Submissions followed by prayer and patience. It wasn't glamorous, but it worked.

Our system became more refined as we went along. We color-coded deadlines. Red for urgent. Yellow for upcoming. Green for distance. We created a master spreadsheet that tracked the name of each scholarship, the deadline, the award amount, the requirements, and the status of our application. When we submitted an application, we noted the date. When we received a response, we updated the status. This level of organization kept us from missing deadlines and helped us see our progress.

I also created a checklist for each application. Essay required? Recommendation letters needed? Transcript? Financial documents? Community service hours? We went through the checklist before submitting anything to make sure we hadn't overlooked a requirement. Missing one document could disqualify an otherwise strong application, and I wasn't willing to let that happen.

What I learned is this. Scholarships aren't rare. They're abundant. The challenge is awareness and follow-through. Many students miss out because they assume they won't qualify or they give up too soon.

I watched this play out time and time again. Parents would start strong, applying for five or ten scholarships. Then they'd hear nothing for weeks and assume it wasn't working. They'd stop applying. What they didn't understand is that scholarship committees often don't make decisions for months. Silence doesn't mean rejection. It usually just means waiting.

I told every parent I worked with the same thing. Don't stop applying just because you haven't heard back yet. Keep moving forward. The awards will come in Yahuah's timing, not yours.

One mother I mentored wanted to quit after her son applied for fifteen scholarships without hearing anything. I told her to keep going. Two months later, five award letters arrived in the same week. Her son ended up with over $13,000 in scholarships. She was overwhelmed with emotion, thanking me for not letting her give up. I told her the persistence was hers, not mine. I had simply reminded her of what she already had inside.

When I speak to parents and students now, I encourage them to look everywhere. Start locally. Ask questions. Use online tools. Talk to employers and community groups. And pray for guidance. Yahuah will lead you to opportunities when you're willing to look.

I also tell them to network. Talk to other parents whose children have gone to college. Ask what scholarships their kids applied for and which ones they won. Most people are willing to share information if you ask. I built relationships with parents whose children were a year or two ahead of mine in school. They gave me insight into scholarships I wouldn't have found on my own.

The church became another valuable resource. Many churches offer scholarships to their members or their members' children. Some are small, $500 or $1,000. Others are more substantial. I made sure my daughters applied for every church scholarship they were eligible for. But I also looked beyond our own congregation. Some denominations and religious organizations offer scholarships that are open to students from any church. I researched those and applied for them as well.

Civic organizations like Rotary, Kiwanis, Lions Club, and Elks Lodge often sponsor scholarships. Many of these organizations are looking for students who demonstrate leadership and service, which fit both of my daughters perfectly. I attended community events where these organizations were present. I introduced myself. I asked about their scholarship programs. I made sure my daughters' names were known.

Alumni associations also offer scholarships. If you or your spouse attended college, check with the alumni association. Many schools offer scholarships to children of alumni. Even if you didn't graduate, some schools still consider you an alumnus if you attended for a certain number of semesters. I reached out to Tuskegee's alumni office and asked about opportunities for my daughters. That connection opened doors.

Professional associations related to your field of work may also offer scholarships. If you're a nurse, check nursing associations. If you're an engineer, check engineering organizations. If you're a teacher, check education groups. These scholarships often go unclaimed because people don't think to look for them.

The more I searched, the more I found. It felt like every organization I encountered had some kind of scholarship program. The key was asking. Most people never ask, so they never find out what's available.

Scholarships aren't hiding. They're waiting. Waiting for someone prepared, persistent, and faithful enough to claim them.

I often think about all the money that goes unclaimed every year because students and families don't know where to look. It frustrates me because the need is so great and the resources are so abundant. The gap between the two is simply information and effort.

That's why I'm so passionate about teaching families how to search. I want to close that gap. I want every family to know that scholarships aren't reserved for a special few. They're available to anyone willing to do the work.

One of my favorite success stories involves a young man named Marcus. His family didn't have much money, and he assumed college was out of reach. His grades were good but not exceptional. He wasn't an athlete. He wasn't involved in many clubs. He thought he had nothing to offer on a scholarship application.

I sat down with him and asked him to tell me about his life. He worked twenty hours a week at a grocery store to help his mother pay bills. He took care of his younger siblings after school while his mother worked a second job. He cooked dinner most nights. He helped his siblings with their homework. He was responsible, dependable, and mature beyond his years.

I told him that his story was powerful. I told him that scholarship committees want to support students like him. Students who overcome obstacles. Students who take responsibility. Students who understand sacrifice.

We worked together to craft essays that told his story honestly. He applied for scholarships focused on first-generation college students, students from low-income families, and students who demonstrated perseverance. He won enough money to cover his first two years of community college. After that, he transferred to a four-year university with additional scholarships and graduated debt-free.

Marcus taught me that every student has a story worth telling. The key is helping them see the value in their own experiences.

When families come to me now feeling discouraged, I remind them of stories like Marcus. I remind them that scholarships exist for all kinds of students. Not just the valedictorian. Not just the star athlete. Not just the student with perfect test scores. Scholarships exist for students who work hard, serve their communities, overcome challenges, and dream big.

Your job is to find the scholarships that match your child's strengths and story. They're out there. You just have to look.

### From the Author's Voice:

*"Scholarships aren't hiding from you; they're hiding FOR you. Yahuah will reveal every opportunity meant for you if you stay faithful and keep looking."*

***

# CHAPTER 4: THE HEART BEHIND THE APPLICATION

*Why Authentic Stories Shine Brighter Than Perfect Grades*

When people ask me what scholarship committees really look for, my answer is always the same. They're looking for stories, not just statistics.

I learned early that grades alone aren't enough. Yes, GPA matters, but it's only one part of the picture. What truly captures attention is the heart behind the application. Committees want to see determination, growth, and purpose reflected in a student's story.

Scholarship committees read hundreds, sometimes thousands, of applications. They see perfect GPAs and high test scores all day long. After a while, the numbers blur together. What stands out is the student who can articulate why they want to learn, what drives them, and how they plan to use their education to make a difference. That's what committees remember. That's what wins scholarships.

Studies of actual scholarship selection rubrics reveal that while GPA typically accounts for only five to ten points out of a possible hundred in scoring systems, essays and character evaluations can be worth fifteen points or more. Many scholarship committees establish minimum academic requirements first, then make their final decisions mainly on the strength of personal statements, letters of recommendation, and demonstrated character. As one scholarship administrator put it, 'your grades get you considered, but your story is what wins the award.'

I understood this instinctively because I'd read enough scholarship descriptions to notice a pattern. Nearly every application asked for an essay or personal statement. If grades were the only thing that mattered, they wouldn't ask students to write. They'd just rank applicants by GPA and call it a day. But they don't do that. They ask for stories because stories reveal character.

When Alayna began applying for scholarships, she had solid grades and was involved in school activities, but I knew we needed to go deeper. I told her, "They want to know who you are, not just what you've done." So we talked through her journey, what motivated her, what challenges she'd faced, and what kind of impact she hoped to make.

At first, Alayna resisted. She thought it was enough to list her accomplishments and let them speak for themselves. She tutored middle school students in math. She'd volunteered at church. She had maintained an honor roll. She thought that was her story. I told her those were facts. Her story was the reason behind the facts.

I asked her why she tutored middle school students. She said because she wanted to help them understand math better. I pushed further. Why did that matter to you? She paused. Then she said, "Because I like helping people see that they're smarter than they think. I like watching them finally understand something they thought was too hard." There it was. That was the heart behind the activity.

We did that with every accomplishment on her resume. Why did you volunteer at church? Why did you tutor younger students? Why does education matter to you? What do you hope to do with your degree? Those conversations became the foundation for her essays. They weren't lists of achievements. They were honest reflections of her faith, work ethic, and desire to help others. That authenticity made her stand out.

One essay prompt asked her to describe a time when she overcame a challenge. She wanted to write about a difficult test she studied for. I told her that was fine, but it didn't reveal much about her character. I asked if there was something deeper. Something that tested her resolve or shaped who she was becoming. She thought about it for a few days. Then she came to me and said she wanted to write about watching me struggle to pay for my education at Tuskegee and having to leave. She said it made her determined to finish what I couldn't.

When she read that essay to me, I cried. It was honest. It was vulnerable. It was her. That essay won her a $3000 scholarship.

Laura's process looked different. Writing about herself didn't come easily. I sat beside her as she stared at a blank screen, unsure where to begin. I told her, "Write like you're talking to me." Once she relaxed, her words began to flow.

But even then, her first drafts weren't ready. Like most students, she started by trying to write what she thought committees wanted to hear. Her early essays were polished but impersonal. They listed accomplishments but didn't reveal character. They stated facts but didn't share the story.

One particular essay transformed completely through revision. The prompt asked students to describe an obstacle they'd overcome and how it shaped them. Laura's first attempt looked like this:

**BEFORE (First Draft — Generic):**

When I moved to a new school district, I faced many academic challenges. The new school had a more advanced curriculum than my previous school. I struggled in my classes, especially math, which had always been my favorite subject.

I was placed in a different math class to catch up with the other students. I did not like being in a lower-level class. I worked hard to improve my grades. Eventually, I was moved back to the regular class.

This experience taught me the importance of hard work and perseverance. I learned that challenges can be overcome with determination. These lessons will help me succeed in college and in my future career.

I read it and saw the problem immediately. Everything she wrote was true, but it was flat. There was no emotion. No detail. No Laura.

"Tell me what it really felt like," I said. "When they put you in that other math class, how did you feel?"

She was quiet for a moment. Then she said, "I felt like I wasn't smart enough. Like I didn't belong."

"Write that," I told her.

"What do you mean?" she asked.

"Write exactly what you just told me. Don't polish it. Don't make it sound impressive. Just tell the truth."

She looked uncertain, but she tried. Over the next few days, we worked through that essay together. I didn't write it for her. I asked questions. I pushed her to go deeper. I reminded her that vulnerability isn't weakness. It's strength.

Here is what she finally submitted:

## AFTER (Final Draft — Authentic):

When I was younger, I had to make a very tough transition from my old home in the inner city of Houston, Texas to my current suburban home in Katy, Texas. This was a huge obstacle for me to overcome because I knew no one and now attended a predominately white school and the curriculum was more advanced than my old school.

When I first made the move, it was hard. I didn't like it nor understand why we had to move in the first place. Every second away from my old life made me miss it so much more.

The hardest part I had to face was the change in schools, not only the making new friends but the advanced curriculum. Katy ISD's curriculum moved at a faster pace than the one in Alief ISD. I found myself making C's and D's in the same classes that I made A's and B's in my old school and especially in the math and science classes, my two favorite subjects. This disturbed me greatly!

I knew I couldn't keep going on like this, just because I didn't like the place didn't mean that I had to settle for what was happening. So I made a decision to buckle down, roll my sleeves up and do my best to learn and adjust to the new school system. I started going to tutorials to understand better. I didn't catch on quick enough to stay in my current class so I was switched to a different math class that basically helped students who were behind to catch up and learn quicker.

This was like a miracle for me because once I got to class I started to understand better and it didn't take long for me to excel to the top of the class. Once I did that, I was allowed to go back to my old class. Not only did it help me but it also made me love math so much more and with that class I also made new friends.

So, my moving to a new city was a big obstacle for me but once I arrived I took the actions needed to tackle the obstacle and it has made me aware that change will happen, I just need to figure out how to adjust to it.

***

The difference was striking. The second version wasn't grammatically perfect. It had some run-on sentences. The punctuation wasn't flawless. But it was real. You could hear Laura's voice. You could feel her frustration. You could see her determination.

When she submitted that essay for a local scholarship focused on perseverance, she won. The scholarship was for $1,500. More importantly, the selection committee commented specifically on her essay. They said her honesty stood out. They said they could tell she'd written it herself, not copied something from the internet or had someone else write it for her.

That confirmation taught Laura something powerful. Being real matters more than being perfect.

The same principle applied to every essay she wrote after that. She stopped trying to impress and started trying to connect. She wrote about tutoring younger students and discovering that teaching helped her learn. She wrote about managing basketball, academics, and family responsibilities and learning that discipline is built one choice at a time. She wrote about her dreams of becoming an accountant not because it sounded prestigious but because she genuinely loved the logic and structure of numbers.

Each essay was honest. Each one revealed something true about who she was. And each one earned respect from scholarship committees because authenticity can't be faked.

I learned something through that process too. My job wasn't to make my daughters sound smarter or more accomplished than they were. My job was to help them find their own voices and trust that their stories were enough.

Laura's strength was consistency. She showed up. She followed through. She kept her commitments. I told her that was a story worth telling. Not every essay has to be about overcoming some dramatic obstacle. Sometimes the story is about being dependable, working hard, and doing what you said you would do, even when no one is watching.

One scholarship asked applicants to describe their work ethic. Laura wrote about balancing school, extracurricular activities, and family responsibilities. She wrote about cooking dinner for the family on nights when I worked late. She wrote about helping her younger cousins with homework. She wrote about the satisfaction she felt when she completed something well, even if no one else noticed. That essay revealed her character in a way that grades never could.

Another scholarship prompt asked about leadership. Laura didn't hold a traditional leadership title like president or captain for most of her high school career. At first, she thought she couldn't answer that question. I told her leadership isn't always about titles. Leadership is about influence. It's about taking responsibility when others won't. It's about helping people become better versions of themselves.

She wrote about being the person her teammates came to when they needed encouragement. She wrote about staying late after practice to help younger players improve their skills. She wrote about speaking up in group projects when no one else wanted to take charge. Those examples showed leadership more powerfully than any title could have.

Over time, I noticed a clear pattern among successful applicants. They were consistent in their efforts. They stayed involved in their communities. They expressed gratitude. Most importantly, they were genuine. Scholarship committees can tell when a story is forced and when it's sincere.

I reviewed applications for other students, and I could always tell which essays were authentic and which ones were written to impress. The authentic ones had specific details. They used real examples. They sounded like the student was talking to you, not performing for you. The essays written to impress used big words and vague statements. They sounded like someone trying too hard to sound smart.

I told every student I worked with to write like they talk. Use your own voice. Don't try to sound like someone else. Committees aren't looking for perfect grammar or fancy vocabulary. They're looking for real people with real stories.

I also learned the importance of preparation. Using the system we'd built, we kept transcripts, resumes, service hours, and recommendation letters ready. When deadlines approached, we weren't scrambling. Organization removed stress and allowed us to focus on quality.

Preparation meant having multiple versions of essays ready to go. Some scholarships asked for 500-word essays. Others wanted 250 words. A few wanted 1,000 words or more. Instead of writing a new essay from scratch every time, we learned to adapt our core stories to fit different word counts and prompts. We kept a master document with all of Alayna's and Laura's essays organized by topic. Leadership. Service. Overcoming challenges. Career goals. Faith. Family. When a new prompt came up, we could pull from that document and adjust as needed.

We also kept a running list of people who'd agreed to write recommendation letters. Teachers. Coaches. Church leaders. Employers. Community mentors. Before asking someone to write a letter, we made sure they knew my daughters well and could speak specifically about their character and accomplishments. A generic letter does more harm than good. A detailed, personal letter can make the difference between winning and losing.

I told my daughters to make it easy for people to help them. When they asked someone for a recommendation letter, they provided a resume, a list of accomplishments, and information about the scholarship they were applying for. They also gave plenty of notice. Asking someone to write a letter with only a few days' notice is disrespectful of their time. We gave at least two weeks, and often more.

We also followed up with thank-you notes, handwritten notes, not emails. When someone took the time to write a letter or fill out a form on behalf of my daughters, we made sure they knew we appreciated it. Gratitude matters. It reflects character, and it makes people more willing to help you again in the future.

Through this process, one truth became clear. Yahuah honors preparation. Every late night, every revision, and every prayer was part of the testimony. Each scholarship earned represented more than financial support. It was proof that faith, effort, and authenticity work together.

One particular scholarship required three essays, two recommendation letters, a transcript, and a video submission. The application took weeks to complete. Alayna was frustrated. She said it was too much work for a scholarship that might not even pan out. I told her that the effort itself was valuable. Every essay she wrote made her a better writer. Every revision taught her to think critically about her own experiences. Whether she won or not, the process was shaping her.

She won that scholarship. It was worth $5,000 and renewable for four years. The total value was $20,000. When the award letter arrived, I reminded her of the conversation we'd had. I told her that Yahuah honors the work we put in, even when we can't see the outcome yet.

Laura had a similar experience with a scholarship that required applicants to submit a portfolio of community service. She had to document every volunteer activity she'd participated in over the past three years, including hours, descriptions, and letters from supervisors. It was tedious. But putting together that portfolio helped her see the impact she'd made. She realized she'd logged over 200 hours of service. She'd tutored elementary students. She'd served meals at a homeless shelter. She'd organized donation drives at church. Seeing it all in one place gave her confidence and reminded her that she had something valuable to offer.

That portfolio won her a scholarship worth $4,000. More importantly, it gave her a sense of pride in what she'd accomplished.

When parents and students ask how to qualify for scholarships, I tell them this. Be diligent. Be organized. Be authentic. And stay faithful. Because in the end, it's not about meeting requirements. It's about walking on purpose and trusting Yahuah to open the right doors at the right time.

I also tell them to start with self-reflection. Before writing any essays, sit down and think about your story. What makes you who you are? What challenges have you faced? What have you learned? What do you care about? What impact do you want to make? Answering those questions honestly will give you material for dozens of essays.

I had my daughters do this exercise before we started applying for scholarships. I gave them a list of questions and told them to write down their answers without worrying about grammar or structure. Just write. Get your thoughts on paper. Some of their answers were a few sentences. Others were a page or more. That raw material became the foundation for every essay they wrote.

Another important lesson I learned is that vulnerability is strength. Students often think they need to present themselves as perfect. They're afraid to talk about struggles or failures because they think it will make them look weak. The opposite is true. Scholarship committees want to see growth. They want to see resilience. They want to know that you can face challenges and come out stronger.

One of Alayna's most powerful essays was about a time she failed. She'd applied for a leadership position at school and didn't get it. She was disappointed and embarrassed. But instead of giving up, she found other ways to lead. She started a study group for students struggling in math. She volunteered to mentor freshmen. She learned that leadership isn't about titles. It's about influence.

That essay won her a leadership scholarship worth $3,000. The committee was impressed by her maturity and her ability to learn from disappointment.

I also encourage students to show gratitude in their essays. Scholarship committees are investing in your future. They want to know that you appreciate the opportunity and that you'll use it wisely. A simple statement of gratitude can go a long way. Thank the committee for considering your application. Express how much the scholarship would mean to you and your family. Acknowledge the impact it would have on your education and future.

Gratitude isn't just good manners. It reflects character. It shows humility. And it makes you memorable.

Looking back on this part of the journey, I'm grateful for every essay my daughters wrote. I'm grateful for every late night we spent refining their stories. I'm grateful for the process itself because it taught them how to articulate their values, their goals, and their purpose.

Those skills served them far beyond scholarship applications. They used them in college admissions essays. They used them in job interviews. They use them now in their careers. The ability to tell your story clearly and authentically is a skill that will open doors for the rest of your life.

## From the Author's Voice:

"Your child's story is their strongest asset. Committees don't want perfect, they want real. Teach them to write from the heart, and the scholarships will follow."

***

# CHAPTER 5: WALKING BESIDE YOUR CHILD

*Turning the Scholarship Search Into a Journey of Faith*

If there was one thing I learned during this journey, it's that scholarships don't happen by chance. They require time, effort, intention, and teamwork. Early on, I realized this wasn't something my daughters could do on their own. It had to become a family mission.

Once I made that decision, everything changed. We stopped approaching scholarships as scattered tasks and started treating them as a shared responsibility. We built a system that worked for us, one that brought order to what could easily feel overwhelming.

Parents often ask me if they should let their children handle the scholarship process independently. They worry about being too involved or hovering too much. I understand that concern, but I tell them this. High school students are still learning how to manage complex tasks. They're developing organizational skills, time management, and follow-through. Expecting them to navigate the scholarship process alone is like expecting them to drive across the country without a map or GPS. They might figure it out eventually, but they'll waste time, miss opportunities, and likely get frustrated enough to quit.

Your role isn't to do the work for them. Your role is to guide, support, and hold them accountable. You're the project manager. They're the lead contributor. Together, you make it happen.

Our system started with organization. We created a scholarship binder that became our command center. Inside it were sections for applications, essays, deadlines, recommendation letters, transcripts, and notes. We used folders to separate opportunities and keep everything accessible. A calendar became essential. Deadlines were color-coded so we could see at a glance what needed attention and when. Every completed task was checked off. Even small progress felt meaningful.

The binder lived on our kitchen table for two solid years. It was the first thing I looked at in the morning and the last thing I checked before bed. My daughters knew where to find everything they needed. If they had a question about a deadline or a requirement, the answer was in the binder.

I also created a master tracking spreadsheet. It listed every scholarship we were pursuing, along with the deadline, the award amount, the requirements, application status, and any notes for follow-up. That spreadsheet gave us a bird's-eye view of where we stood at any given moment. We could see which applications were complete, which ones were in progress, and which ones were coming up next.

## The Scholarship Tracking System That Saved Us

Let me walk you through exactly how we set up our system, because this made all the difference between staying organized and drowning in paperwork.

The binder itself was a three-inch, three-ring binder with clear sheet protectors and tabbed dividers. I labeled five main sections. Applied. Submitted. Pending. Won. Rejected. Every scholarship moved through these tabs as we progressed.

In the Applied section, I kept copies of blank applications we were considering. If I found a scholarship online or heard about one at church, I printed the requirements and filed them there. This section was always the fullest because we were constantly adding new opportunities.

Once we completed an application and sent it off, I moved everything to the Submitted section. I kept copies of what we sent, confirmation emails, and notes about submission dates. This way, if a scholarship committee ever claimed they didn't receive something, we had proof of submission.

The Pending section held applications we'd started but not finished. Maybe we were waiting for a recommendation letter. Maybe the essay needed more work. Maybe the deadline was still weeks away. Keeping these separate from completed work helped us stay focused on what still needed attention.

When an award letter arrived, I moved that scholarship to the Won section. I kept the award letter, acceptance documents, and disbursement instructions all together.

Seeing this section grow thicker was one of the most encouraging parts of the process.

The Rejected section existed for a reason. Every rejection letter went here as a reminder that no doesn't mean stop. It means keep going. Looking at this section alongside the Won section always puts things in perspective.

I also kept a separate section at the front of the binder for master documents. Five copies of official transcripts. Ten copies of Alayna's resume. Ten copies of Laura's resume. A list of recommendation letter writers with their contact information. Personal statements we could adapt for different prompts. Having these ready to go meant we never scrambled at the last minute.

The spreadsheet was just as important as the binder. I created it in Excel with seven columns. Scholarship Name. Deadline. Essay Required. Award Amount. Status. Notes. Date Submitted.

Under Scholarship Name, I wrote the full name of the scholarship and the organization offering it. Under Deadline, I listed the date and highlighted it in the color that matched our calendar system. Under Essay Required, I wrote yes or no, and if yes, I noted the word count. Under Award Amount, I listed what the scholarship was worth and whether it was one-time or renewable. Under Status, I tracked where we were: Not Started, In Progress, Submitted, Awarded or Rejected. Under Notes, I wrote anything important. Requires two recommendation letters. I need financial documents.

Interview required. Under Date Submitted, I recorded when we sent the application.

Every Sunday during our scholarship sessions, we reviewed that spreadsheet line by line. We updated statuses. We added new opportunities. We checked upcoming deadlines. That spreadsheet became our roadmap.

The calendar method was simple but effective. I bought a large wall calendar and hung it in the kitchen where everyone could see it. Every scholarship deadline was marked. I used colored markers to code them by month. Red for deadlines within two weeks. Yellow for deadlines two to four weeks out. Green for deadlines more than a month away. At a glance, we could see what needed immediate attention and what could wait.

I also kept a filing box specifically for recommendation letters and transcripts. Each teacher or mentor who agreed to write a letter had their own folder. Inside, I kept copies of the letters they wrote, notes about which scholarships they supported, and thank-you cards we sent. This way, we never asked the same person for too many letters in a short period, and we always knew who to approach for specific types of scholarships.

Transcripts were stored in a separate folder, organized by date. Every time we requested an official transcript from the school, I noted when it was ordered, when it arrived, and how many copies we had on hand. Running out of transcripts during a busy application season would've been a disaster, so I always kept extras.

This system wasn't complicated, but it was thorough. It removed guesswork. It eliminated panic. It gave us control over a process that could easily have controlled us.

That structure gave us clarity. Instead of reacting to deadlines, we planned for them. Instead of scrambling, we prepared. Organization removed stress and allowed us to focus on doing quality work.

I learned that good organization isn't just about staying on top of deadlines. It's about creating a system that reduces anxiety. When everything is organized, you can see the path forward. When things are chaotic, every deadline feels like an emergency. Our system eliminated that chaos. We knew what was coming. We knew what we needed to do. We could work steadily instead of constantly putting out fires.

The spreadsheet became especially valuable when multiple scholarships had overlapping deadlines. We could look ahead two or three weeks and see what was coming. If we had three scholarships due the same week, we started working on them early so we weren't rushing at the last minute. Planning ahead gave us control over the process instead of letting the process control us.

My daughters took ownership of their applications, but they always knew they were supported. I became the editor and encourager, reviewing essays, asking questions, and helping them refine their thoughts. We talked through clarity and tone, making sure their voices came through honestly. Some evenings we sat at the kitchen table for hours, reading sentences aloud and polishing ideas until they felt right.

One night, Alayna and I worked on an essay about her faith journey. She'd written a solid draft, but something felt off. I read it aloud to her, and we both realized the problem. She was trying to sound impressive instead of being herself. I told her to start over. Write what you really believe, I said. Don't worry about impressing anyone. Just tell the truth.

She rewrote the essay, and the difference was night and day. The new version was vulnerable, honest, and powerful. That essay won her a faith-based scholarship worth $2,000. The lesson was clear. Authenticity always wins.

My husband was part of the mission as well. He reviewed transcripts, double-checked forms, and handled practical details we couldn't afford to miss. He made sure everything was accurate before submission. Those behind-the-scenes efforts mattered. We were working as a unit.

My husband also played another important role. He kept me grounded. There were times when I became so focused on scholarships that I forgot to celebrate other things happening in our daughters' lives. He'd remind me that they were still teenagers. They still needed time to be kids. They still needed to hang out with friends, go to football games, and enjoy their senior year. Balance mattered, and he made sure we maintained it.

I'm grateful for his perspective. Without it, I might have pushed everyone too hard. I might have turned the scholarship process into a burden instead of a journey. He reminded me to keep things in perspective and to celebrate the small joys along the way.

We also created routines. We set aside regular times each week to search for scholarships, work on essays, and review progress. Sometimes it was a quiet weekend afternoon. Other times it was a late evening after dinner. The schedule was flexible, but the commitment was firm. That consistency built discipline and momentum.

Sunday afternoons became our dedicated scholarship time. After church and lunch, we'd gather at the dining room table with our laptops, the binder, and our tracking spreadsheet. We'd review what was due in the coming weeks, discuss which scholarships to prioritize, and divide up the tasks. Alayna might work on an essay while Laura updated her resume. I'd research new opportunities and add them to the list. My husband would review completed applications to make sure we hadn't missed anything.

Those Sunday sessions became sacred time. We protected them. We didn't schedule other activities during that time. We didn't let distractions pull us away. It was our time to work together toward a shared goal.

Sometimes friends or extended family didn't understand why we were so strict about protecting that time. They'd invite us to events or ask us to do things on Sunday afternoons. I politely declined and explained that we had a standing commitment. Some people thought I was being too rigid. But I knew that consistency was the key to our success. If we skipped one week, it'd be easier to skip the next. Before long, we'd lose momentum entirely.

There were nights when exhaustion set in. After long workdays, the last thing I wanted to do was review another essay or track another deadline. But then I'd remember why we were doing this. This wasn't **busy work**. It was an investment. Every late night was a seed planted for the future.

I also learned to recognize when my daughters needed a break. Pushing too hard can lead to burnout. There were weeks when we backed off and gave them space to rest. A sustainable pace matters more than short bursts of intense effort. This was a marathon, not a sprint.

One week, Laura told me she was tired. She said she needed a break from essays and applications. I could see the exhaustion in her face. Instead of pushing, I told her to take the week off. No scholarship work. Just rest. She was surprised, but relieved. The following week, she came back refreshed and ready to work. That break made her more productive in the long run.

Recognizing when to push and when to pause became an important skill. I had to pay attention to my daughters' emotional and mental state. If they were burned out, forcing them to keep going would only lead to resentment and poor-quality work. Giving them permission to rest when they needed it showed them that I cared about them, not just about the results.

Prayer became part of our rhythm. Before submitting major applications, we paused and prayed together. I'd say, "We've done our part. Now we trust Yahuah to do His." That practice grounded us. It reminded us that effort and faith are meant to work together.

I also learned that teamwork extends beyond the home. Teachers, mentors, and church leaders became part of our support system. They wrote recommendation letters, offered feedback, and spoke encouragement when we needed it most. Hearing positive feedback from people who saw my daughters outside our home affirmed that the discipline we practiced daily was making a difference.

One teacher in particular became a tremendous advocate for Alayna. Mrs. Columbine taught her junior and senior year chemistry classes and saw something special in her analytical thinking. Mrs. Columbine, who held both a B.S. and a master's degree in chemical engineering, encouraged Alayna to pursue STEM scholarships and apply for programs that valued scientific reasoning. She wrote multiple recommendation letters and never complained about the requests. She even offered to review essays before they were submitted. Mrs. Columbine believed in Alayna, and that belief made a difference.

Laura had a similar relationship with her junior and senior year accounting teacher, Mrs. Onieon. She recognized Laura's exceptional talent for accounting and was so impressed that she convinced the school to offer an Accounting II course that had never been part of the curriculum. Laura was the only student who signed up for the class, which meant she was essentially teaching herself with guidance from Mrs. Onieon. That's how strongly her teacher believed in her potential and wanted her to pursue accounting in college. She even secured Laura a paid summer internship while she was still in high school, working as an accounting intern with no college experience. Her support opened doors for Laura that she might not have pursued on her own.

These teachers weren't just educators. They were mentors. They invested in my daughters beyond the classroom, and we were deeply grateful for their involvement.

Building relationships with teachers also required effort on our part. We didn't just ask for favors. We showed appreciation. We kept them updated on outcomes. When Alayna won a scholarship that Mrs. Columbine had supported, we made sure she knew about it. We brought her a thank-you card and a small gift. We wanted her to know that her investment mattered.

Just as important as organization was emotional support. Rejection letters can sting, even when you know they're part of the process. When discouragement crept in, we paused. We took a breath. We prayed. Then we moved forward. I reminded my daughters often, "Every no brings us closer to the right yes."

I kept a folder of rejection letters. Not to dwell on them, but to remind us that rejection is part of the process. Every successful person has been rejected. Every scholarship winner has also been told no. The difference between those who succeed and those who quit is persistence.

One day, after Alayna received three rejection letters in the same week, she came to me frustrated. She said, "Mama, I'm working so hard and getting nothing." I pulled out the folder of rejections and spread them across the table. Then I pulled out the folder of acceptance letters and spread those out too. I told her to look at both. The acceptances outnumbered the rejections. The money we'd received far exceeded what we'd been denied. Rejection is loud, but success is louder if you keep going.

That visual reminder shifted her perspective. She realized she'd been focusing on the losses instead of the wins. From that day forward, she approached rejection differently. It became data, not defeat.

The reality of scholarship rejection rates helps put the process in perspective. The Coca-Cola Scholars Program receives over 103,000 applications annually and awards only 150 scholarships, representing a selection rate of just 0.15%. The Gates Scholarship sees similar odds, with roughly 34,000 applicants competing for 300 awards, a 0.9% acceptance rate. Even less competitive scholarships typically have selection rates between 10–12%. Students who successfully fund their education through scholarships average one award for every eight to ten applications submitted. Understanding these odds helps families recognize that rejection isn't personal failure but a mathematical reality of a competitive process.

There was a night during Laura's senior year when she broke down. She'd been rejected from two scholarships in one week. Awards she'd worked hard on; essays she'd poured her heart into. I watched the mail pile up on the counter, each envelope another no.

She sat at the kitchen table with her head in her hands and said, "Mama, what if this doesn't work? What if I'm not good enough?"

My heart broke for her. I could see the exhaustion on her face, the doubt creeping in. But I couldn't let her quit. Not when we'd come this far. Not when I knew what Yahuah could do.

I sat beside her and took her hand. "Baby, those no's don't mean you're not good enough. They just mean Yahuah has something better waiting."

She looked up at me, visibly upset. "But what if there isn't anything better? What if this is it?"

"Then we keep going," I said. "We keep applying. We keep trusting. Because giving up guarantees we won't see what Yahuah has planned."

We prayed together that night. Right there at the kitchen table with rejection letters spread between us. I reminded her of every win we'd already seen. Every letter that had come through. Every door that had opened. Every time Yahuah had shown up when we needed Him most.

I told her, "We're not stopping now. We're going to keep applying, and we're going to trust that Yahuah's timing is perfect."

She nodded, wiping her tears. The doubt was still there, but so was a flicker of determination.

Two weeks later, she received a scholarship. It didn't equal the total of those three rejections, but it confirmed that her efforts were paying off. When she opened the letter and saw the amount, she ran to find me. We hugged in the kitchen and celebrated. Not because it was a large award, but because it was confirmation that Yahuah was still moving on her behalf.

Sometimes Yahuah allows us to face disappointment so the blessing feels even sweeter when it arrives. The valley makes the mountaintop more meaningful. The waiting makes the answer more precious.

Laura learned something that night too. She learned that doubt doesn't disqualify you. Discouragement doesn't mean you're on the wrong path. Sometimes it just means you're being tested, and the breakthrough is closer than you think.

We learned to celebrate progress, not just outcomes. Completing an application mattered. Submitting an essay on time mattered. Every step forward deserved acknowledgment. When award letters arrived, we celebrated with gratitude. When they didn't, we regrouped and kept going. Each experience built resilience.

I made it a point to celebrate every completed application, regardless of the outcome. When my daughters finished an essay or submitted a scholarship application, we acknowledged it. Sometimes the celebration was simple. A high five. A word of encouragement. Other times, we did something special: Ice cream, a movie night, or a break from scholarship work. The point was to recognize effort, not just results.

This approach taught my daughters that success isn't just about winning. It's about showing up, doing your best, and trusting the process. That mindset served them well beyond scholarships. It shaped how they approached challenges in college and in their careers.

One of the most important lessons I learned is that teamwork builds endurance. When one person feels tired, another steps in to lift them up. Shared purpose pushes back discouragement. Families win scholarships together.

There were weeks when I was exhausted and ready to give up. During those times, my husband would take over. He'd sit with the girls and review their work. He'd encourage them when I didn't have the energy. There were also times when my daughters encouraged me. They reminded me of how far we had come. They'd thank me for not giving up on them. That mutual support kept us moving forward.

Teamwork also meant being honest about struggles. When something wasn't working, we talked about it. When deadlines felt overwhelming, we adjusted our approach. When we needed help, we asked for it. Open communication prevented resentment and kept us aligned.

If I had to sum up this part of the journey, I'd say it's preparation mixed with persistence and fueled by purpose. It's not easy, but it's possible when families commit to walking through the process side by side.

I often tell parents that the scholarship process will test you. It'll test your patience. It'll test your organization. It'll test your commitment. But it'll also strengthen your family. It'll teach your children discipline, resilience, and faith. It'll create memories and conversations that last long after the scholarships are awarded.

Looking back, some of my most treasured memories are from those nights at the kitchen table. Working together. Praying together. Celebrating together. The scholarships were the goal, but the journey brought us closer as a family.

Scholarships aren't earned through applications alone. They're earned through commitment, consistency, faith, and a family willing to stay engaged until the work is done. When you approach it as a team, the process becomes less about pressure and more about purpose. The late nights become investments. The rejections become lessons. The successes become testimonies.

And when your child walks across that stage to receive their diploma, debt-free and full of confidence, you'll look back and realize that every moment was worth it. Every sacrifice. Every prayer. Every late night. It all mattered. Because you didn't just help your child pay for college. You taught them how to dream, how to work, and how to trust Yahuah with their future.

That's the legacy of this process. Not just the scholarships earned, but the lessons learned. Not just the money saved, but the character built. Not just the degrees obtained, but the faith strengthened.

Years from now, when my daughters face other challenges, they'll draw on what they learned during this season. They'll remember that hard work pays off. They'll remember that persistence overcomes obstacles. They'll remember that family stands together. They'll remember that Yahuah provides when we do our part and trust Him with the rest.

That's what makes this journey so much more than a financial strategy. It's a faith journey. A family journey. A journey that shapes who your children become and prepares them for everything that lies ahead.

### *From the Author's Voice:*

"This isn't a solo journey. The parent guides. The student works. Yahuah provides. Together, scholarships become inevitable."

***

# PART II: THE SCHOLARSHIP STRATEGY

74

# CHAPTER 6: THE BLESSING OF STRATEGY



*How Wisdom and Faith Make College Affordable*

By the time I began helping other families, I already knew one thing for sure. Scholarships weren't about luck. They were about awareness, preparation, and persistence. What most families needed wasn't talent or perfection. They needed someone to show them where to look and how to stay the course.

One of the first families I worked with outside my own was Monica and her two children, Caleb and Renee.

Monica reached out to me at a moment many parents know too well. College was approaching fast, deadlines were piling up, and the numbers were overwhelming. She told me she was losing sleep trying to figure out how she'd afford it all. I recognized that fear immediately because I'd lived it.

I told her the same thing I'd once told myself. Don't panic. Let's start where we are.

We sat at my dining room table with laptops, notebooks, and stacks of paper. I showed her how to search strategically, how to organize deadlines, and how to help her children tell their stories honestly. I explained that scholarships should be treated like part-time jobs. Consistency mattered more than perfection.

Monica listened carefully. She took notes. She asked questions. I could see the shift happening in her as we talked. The panic in her eyes began to fade, replaced by something else. Focus. Determination. Hope.

I walked her through the same binder system I used with my daughters. I showed her the tracking spreadsheet. I explained how to color-code deadlines and how to keep documents organized. I gave her a list of scholarship websites to start with and a schedule for approaching the work without getting overwhelmed.

Before she left that day, I told her something important. You're not behind. You're right where you need to be. Starting today is better than starting tomorrow, and starting tomorrow is better than never starting at all.

Monica took it seriously. She kept detailed notes, followed up on every deadline, and made sure Caleb and Renee stayed engaged. There were moments when they felt discouraged, especially after weeks of silence from scholarship committees. Monica never let them quit. She reminded them why they started and prayed with them through the waiting.

She called me several times during the process. Sometimes she had questions about specific applications. Other times she just needed encouragement. I always made time for her because I knew what she was feeling. The doubt. The exhaustion. I'm wondering if it was all worth it. I'd been there, and I wanted her to know she wasn't alone.

One conversation in particular stands out. Monica called me late one evening, almost in tears. Caleb had just received his fourth rejection letter in two weeks. She said he was ready to quit. He told her that all the work was for nothing and that maybe college wasn't meant for him. I could hear the fear in her voice. She was afraid he'd give up, and she didn't know how to encourage him.

I told her to put Caleb on the phone. When he got on the line, I asked him a simple question. How many applications have you submitted? He said fifteen. I asked how many rejections he'd received. He said seven. I told him to do the math. That meant eight applications were still out there waiting for a response. I reminded him that most scholarships don't notify applicants for weeks or even months. Silence doesn't mean no. It just means not yet.

Then I told him something else. Every successful person you admire has been rejected more times than you can count. The difference between them and everyone else is that they didn't quit. I told him that if he quit now, he was guaranteeing failure. But if he kept going, he was giving himself a chance at success.

That conversation turned things around for Caleb. He went back to work. Three weeks later, he received his first acceptance. Then another. Then another. By the time the school year ended, he'd won four scholarships totaling over $13,000.

Caleb discovered early on that leadership was his strongest asset. He'd spent time volunteering with younger students and mentoring in his community. We shaped his essays around service, responsibility, and character. One weekend, he applied for a local scholarship that required a personal essay about integrity. Most students skipped it because it took more effort.

The essay prompt asked applicants to describe a time when they demonstrated integrity even when no one was watching. Many students probably read that prompt and moved on to easier applications. But Caleb took the time to think about it. He wrote about finding a wallet in the school parking lot with over $1,000 inside. Instead of keeping it, he turned it into the office. The owner was a janitor at the school who'd just cashed his paycheck. When the man came to claim his wallet, he was overwhelmed with gratitude. He thanked Caleb and told him that money was meant to cover his rent.

Caleb wrote about how that moment changed him. He realized that doing the right thing isn't about recognition or reward. It's about character. It's about who you are when no one is looking.

Caleb was the only applicant. He won.

When Monica called to tell me, her voice cracked with emotion. She said, "Abbie, nobody else even applied." I smiled and told her, "That's what happens when you're willing to do what others won't."

That scholarship was worth $2,000, but the lesson was worth more. Caleb learned that effort matters. That standing out doesn't always mean being the smartest or the most talented. Sometimes it simply means being willing to do the work others avoid.

Caleb also found success with a creative scholarship that many students overlooked. It focused on personal expression rather than grades alone. The scholarship asked applicants to submit a creative project that represented their journey. It could be a video, a piece of art, a written essay, a song, anything that expressed who they were. Most students skipped it because it required more thought and effort than a standard application.

Caleb created short videos in which he talked about his experiences growing up, the challenges his family had faced, and his dreams for the future. He was honest. He was vulnerable. He didn't try to make his life sound more impressive than it was. He just told his truth. That video submission brought in additional scholarship funds that contributed to his overall success.

Renee's journey unfolded differently. She was steady. Dependable. She maintained solid grades, volunteered faithfully, and showed up wherever she committed. Her scholarships reflected that consistency. Leadership awards came. Academic awards followed. Community-based support arrived. One letter after another.

Renee didn't have one standout moment or accomplishment that defined her. Instead, she had years of showing up, doing her best, and serving others. Her essays reflected that consistency. She wrote about the small, faithful actions that most people overlook. Tutoring the same student every week for an entire school year. Volunteering at the food bank every Saturday morning without fail. Keeping her commitments even when it was inconvenient.

Scholarship committees recognized that consistency. They saw a student who'd finish what she started. They saw someone who understood that success isn't built on one big moment, but on a thousand small decisions to do the right thing.

One of Renee's essays talked about commitment. The prompt asked her to describe what commitment meant to her. She could've written something generic about dedication or perseverance. Instead, she wrote about a specific commitment she made to tutor a third grader named Eli who was struggling with reading.

Renee committed to meet with Eli every Tuesday and Thursday afternoon for the entire school year. There were days when she didn't feel like going. Days when she had homework piling up or when her friends were hanging out. But she went anyway because she'd made a promise. By the end of the year, Eli had improved by two grade levels in reading. His mother was overwhelmed with gratitude when she thanked Renee.

Renee wrote about how that experience taught her that commitment isn't about what you do when it's convenient.

It's about what you do when it's hard. That essay won her a scholarship worth $2,500.

The night Monica called and said, "We're going to make this work. We can actually afford to send them both to college," I sat quietly after we hung up and thanked Yahuah. Not just for the money, but for the confirmation. This works when you work it.

Monica's family received over $60,000 in scholarships combined. Caleb's awards covered most of his tuition at a state university. Renee's scholarships paid for her entire first two years at a community college before she transferred to a four-year school. While the scholarships didn't cover everything and they still needed some financial aid and modest loans, they made college affordable and achievable for both children.

Monica became one of my biggest advocates. She told everyone she knew about what we'd accomplished together. She referred other families to me. She volunteered to help at my workshops. She became living proof that the process works for anyone willing to commit.

She also started mentoring other parents in her community. She'd invite them over to her house and show them her own binder system. She shared the tracking spreadsheet I'd given her. She walked them through the process the same way I'd walked her through it. Watching her pay it forward filled my heart. This journey isn't about hoarding knowledge. It's about multiplying it.

One lesson Monica learned early became one of her most powerful teaching tools when helping other families. She learned that comparing costs properly can save tens of thousands of dollars. Many parents look at tuition and assume that's the total cost. It's not. The real cost includes everything.

I showed Monica how to create a true cost comparison when Renee was deciding between schools. School A looked affordable at $18,000 per year for tuition. But when we added room and board at $12,000, meal plans at $4,000, books at $1,200, and fees at $2,000, the real cost was $37,200 annually. Over four years, that was $148,800.

School B had a higher sticker price of $28,000 for tuition. At first glance, it seemed more expensive. But Renee's scholarship package covered $25,000 per year. Her actual cost was $3,000 per year for tuition, plus room and board. When we calculated the total four-year cost, it came to $60,000.

That spreadsheet saved them $88,800. Strategy has power.

Monica started showing that comparison to every parent she mentored. She'd pull out the numbers and walk them through the math. I watched my parents' eyes widen when they saw the difference. Many had been ready to choose schools based on the tuition number alone. They hadn't considered the full picture. Monica's spreadsheet changed how they made decisions.

Good mentoring doesn't just teach the process. It teaches people how to think strategically about every choice. Monica understood that, and she used what she learned to help others avoid costly mistakes.

Around that same time, my dear friend Barbara contacted me about her goddaughter, Sani.

Barbara had been watching what happened with my daughters and Monica's family. She believed the same process could work for Sani, and I agreed to help.

I shared what I knew about the scholarship process with Barbara. I gave her the same tools and strategies I'd used before. Barbara listened carefully and put it into action.

They applied and won the Alpha Phi Alpha Fraternity scholarship. Barbara knew someone who was a member of the organization. Dr. Sterling, a family friend, wrote a letter of recommendation. I'd emphasized the importance of strategic connections. Use people you know who are already connected to the organizations you're applying to.

They also received the Pascagoula Negro Carver High Wall of Fame scholarship. Barbara used her uncle, a retired U.S Navy Colonel, as a reference. Of all the scholarships they applied for, the Wall of Fame was the only renewable one. Sani receives it once a year as long as she stays enrolled and meets the qualifications.

Another scholarship came through Sani's university. In the guidance I provide, I emphasize connecting with administrators and people in the school system. That doesn't stop at high school. Barbara continued reaching out even after Sani started college, asking the counselor about new opportunities.

One day, the counselor called Barbara. She had a scholarship requiring a 1,000-word essay. Nobody wanted to apply for it. Barbara requested for the information. They were the only applicants. The scholarship offered up to $2,000, and because Sani was the only student who applied from all the school districts, they gave her more than the standard $1,000 per student.

They received quite a few scholarships because they followed instructions exactly as written. That was no accident. Barbara made it a point to follow every step of the process the way it was designed to be followed. One scholarship coordinator told her they received about 50 applicants, but only four or five actually included everything requested in the proper format. The committees design requirements that way intentionally. Students heading to college need to follow instructions precisely.

Barbara highlighted requirements in each application, gathered everything needed, and kept it organized. The process went smoothly.

In total, Sani was awarded over $12,000 in scholarships. Not enough to cover everything, but enough to make college affordable when combined with financial aid and grants.

Each time Barbara called with an update, her excitement reminded me of my own daughters opening their first award letters. That same mixture of disbelief and gratitude. That same realization that effort, prayer, and preparation truly pay off.

Barbara was so impressed with the process and the results that she invited me to present the scholarship process at her church. She wanted other families to have the same opportunity that she and Sani had. That invitation opened a door to reach even more families who needed this information.

I knew Sani's confidence grew as the awards came in. It wasn't that she doubted herself before, but each scholarship affirmed what was already inside her. She began to see herself with greater clarity, recognizing her own strength and potential. Capable. Worthy. Chosen.

People often overlook this truth: scholarships do more than pay bills. They change how students see themselves.

Sani started this journey uncertain and overwhelmed. She ended it believing in herself and her future. Every scholarship she won reinforced that belief. She carried herself differently. She spoke with more confidence. She made plans for her future with excitement instead of fear.

When Sani graduated and headed off to college, Barbara called me. She said, "Abbie, I don't know how to thank you." I told her the thanks belonged to them. They did the work. They wrote the essays. They submitted the applications. I just showed them the path. They walked it. And they kept walking it. Scholarships don't stop at high school graduation. As long as you're enrolled and meeting the requirements, opportunities are still available. Barbara and Sani proved that.

By the time both families completed their journeys, I understood something clearly. What started as my personal mission had become something larger. These weren't isolated wins. They were evidence.

Evidence that scholarships are available.

Evidence that faith paired with action produces results.

Evidence that when families stay engaged, doors open.

These stories were never meant to be repeated over and over throughout this book. They were meant to stand here, fully told, as proof that the process works.

If it worked for Monica and her children. If it worked for Barbara and Sani. If it worked for my daughters. It can work for you too.

I continued to help other families after Monica and Barbara. Each one taught me something new. I learned that every family's situation is unique, but the principles remain the same. Start where you are. Stay consistent. Be authentic. Trust the process. Lean on faith.

One family I worked with had three children all within four years of each other in school. The parents were overwhelmed at the thought of paying for three college educations almost simultaneously. I showed them how to stagger applications so they weren't doing everything at once. The oldest child started applying two years before graduation. The middle child started a year later. By the time the youngest was ready, the family had a well-oiled system in place. All three children received enough scholarships to make college affordable.

Another family I helped had a son with learning disabilities. He'd struggled academically but excelled in hands-on learning. His GPA wasn't competitive for most merit scholarships, but we found scholarships specifically for students pursuing vocational training and technical careers. He received funding to attend a trade school where he studied welding. Today, he owns his own small business and earns more money than many of his peers who went to four-year universities.

His story reminded me that college isn't the only path to success. Scholarships exist for trade schools, vocational programs, and certificate programs too. I experienced this firsthand when I received a scholarship for an online course in plant-based nutrition at Cornell University. That opportunity reminded me that scholarships aren't just for young students heading off to college. They're available for anyone committed to learning and growing. Too many families assume scholarships are only for students attending four-year universities. That's not true. There's funding available for all kinds of post-secondary education.

Every family reminded me that there's no one-size-fits-all approach. What works for one student may not work for another. But the fundamentals never change. Do the work. Stay organized. Tell your story. Trust Yahuah.

I also learned that my role wasn't to do the work for families, but to empower them to do it themselves. I gave them tools.

I gave them confidence. I gave them a roadmap. But they had to walk the path.

Some families took what I taught them and ran with it. Others needed more hand-holding. A few gave up when the process got hard. I learned to accept that I couldn't save everyone. I could only help those who were willing to help themselves.

But the families who committed, who stayed consistent, who trusted the process, they won. Every single one of them secured enough funding to make college a reality.

Looking back on those early families, I see Yahuah's hand in every story. He brought Monica to my table at the exact right time. He connected me with Barbara and Sani when they needed help most. He used my experience to bless others, and in doing so, He confirmed my calling.

This wasn't just about scholarships. It was about obedience. It was about stewardship. It was about taking what Yahuah had given me and multiplying it by pouring it into others.

The more families I helped, the more I realized this work wasn't just changing their lives. It was changing mine. Every success story strengthened my faith. Every breakthrough reminded me that Yahuah is faithful. Every family that crossed the finish line with affordable college options was proof that His promises are true.

### From the Author's Voice:

*"Strategy turns hope into results. One spreadsheet, one cost comparison, one wise decision can save your family tens of thousands of dollars. Don't just pray for provision, plan for it."*

***

# CHAPTER 7: THE UNCLAIMED BLESSING

———— ♦ ————

*Finding the Opportunities Others Overlook*

One night, long after everyone had gone to bed, I sat scrolling through scholarship databases online. I'd already bookmarked dozens of opportunities when something stopped me. An article mentioned that millions of dollars in scholarships go unclaimed every single year.

I stared at the screen, reading that sentence over and over again. Unclaimed. How could that be?

According to the National Scholarship Providers Association, approximately $100 million in private scholarships go unawarded each year, not the billions often claimed in popular articles. That widely repeated billions figure actually originated from a misreading of 1970s data about employer tuition benefits, not scholarships. The real issue isn't billions sitting unclaimed, but rather the hundreds of millions in federal Pell Grants that go unused each year because students don't file the FAFSA. For the high school class of 2022 alone, an estimated $3.6 billion in Pell Grant funding went unclaimed. Students miss out on available money primarily because they don't know scholarships exist, assume they wouldn't be competitive, feel intimidated by application requirements, or give up too soon in the process.

It didn't make sense at first. Families were struggling to afford college. Students were giving up on their dreams because of money. And yet, right alongside all of that need, scholarship funds were sitting untouched. I felt frustration rise, followed closely by determination. Right then, I made up my mind. My family wouldn't be among those who overlooked it.

The article explained that scholarships go unclaimed for several reasons. Some have very specific eligibility requirements that limit the applicant pool. Others require extra effort like essays, interviews, or creative submissions that discourage students from applying. Some scholarships receive so few applications that they go unawarded entirely. In some cases, organizations budget money for scholarships but receive no applications at all.

I couldn't believe what I was reading. Organizations were setting aside money specifically to help students, and nobody was claiming it. The gap between need and resources wasn't a shortage of money. It was a shortage of information and effort.

The more I researched, the clearer it became. Many scholarships go unawarded simply because people don't know they exist. Others require essays, interviews, or recommendations that students feel unprepared to complete. Some miss deadlines. Some assume they won't qualify. I realized that what stood between most students and scholarship money wasn't intelligence or talent. It was awareness, confidence, and persistence.

That realization shifted my mindset completely. From that moment forward, I made it my mission to search for overlooked opportunities. I told my daughters, "We're going after the money that others leave behind." And that's exactly what we did.

We applied for scholarships connected to every part of their lives. Academics. Leadership. Community service. Faith-based organizations. Creative interests. Some applications required hours of research and thoughtful writing. Others took only a few minutes to submit. Every single one mattered. I reminded my daughters that each application was a seed planted. Even if we never heard back, Yahuah would honor the effort in His time.

I started looking for scholarships that others overlooked because they seemed too small, too specific, or too much work. A scholarship for $500 might not sound like much compared to a $10,000 award, but $500 is still $500 we didn't have before. And several small scholarships can add up quickly.

One scholarship I found online was called HBCU Tier 3. The application was simple. A one-page form and a short essay about attending an HBCU. The award was only $1,000. Most students probably ignored it because the amount seemed insignificant. But Alayna applied. She wrote about her passion for attending a historically Black college or university and what that opportunity meant to her heritage and future. She was one of three applicants. She won.

That $1,000 taught us an important lesson. Don't judge opportunities by their size. Judge them by whether they're achievable. A small scholarship with little competition is often a better investment of time than a large scholarship with thousands of applicants.

We also applied for scholarships with unusual requirements. One asked students to submit a video explaining why they deserved the scholarship. Most students skipped it because making a video seemed intimidating. Laura decided to try. She recorded herself on her phone speaking about her goals and her gratitude for the opportunity. The video wasn't professionally produced. It was just her, speaking from the heart. She won $1,500.

Another scholarship asked for a creative submission. Students could submit art, poetry, music, or any form of creative expression that represented their journey. Many students ignored it because they didn't consider themselves creative. But I encouraged both of my daughters to think outside the box. Alayna wrote a poem about faith and perseverance. Laura created a photo collage representing her high school experience. One submission won an award.

These experiences confirmed what I'd learned. The scholarships others ignore are often the easiest to win. Not because they require less talent, but because they require more effort. And most people aren't willing to put in that effort.

As I continued helping others, I shared this same truth. I encouraged students to apply for scholarships that seemed small, unusual, or less popular. Many of those opportunities existed precisely because fewer people were willing to put in the effort. Time and again, I watched students succeed simply because they were willing to apply where others wouldn't.

I worked with a young lady named Brittany who was intimidated by scholarships that required creative submissions. She said she wasn't artistic and didn't know what to create. I told her that creativity isn't just about art. It's about expressing yourself authentically.

Brittany loved to bake. She'd learned from her grandmother and spent hours in the kitchen perfecting recipes. I suggested she apply for a scholarship that asked students to submit something representing their passion. She created a photo essay showing herself baking with her grandmother, along with a written reflection about how baking taught her patience, precision, and the importance of family traditions.

She won. The scholarship was worth $2,000. She called me with such excitement and gratitude, thanking me for pushing her to see creativity differently. I told her the creativity was always there. She just needed permission to express it in her own way.

This chapter of the journey taught me something important. Scholarships aren't scarce. They're abundant. The challenge is that many people stop looking too soon. They assume the money is gone, the competition is too strong, or the process is too hard. But persistence changes everything.

I saw this pattern repeat itself over and over. A student would apply for ten scholarships, hear nothing for weeks, and conclude that scholarships weren't for them. They'd stop applying. What they didn't realize is that most scholarship decisions take months. The silence wasn't rejection. It was just timing.

I told every student and parent I worked with the same thing. Don't stop applying just because you haven't heard back yet. Keep submitting. Keep searching. Keep believing that your breakthrough is coming.

One father I mentored wanted to quit after his daughter applied for twenty scholarships without receiving a single award. He said the process was a waste of time. I told him to give it two more months. Within those two months, six award letters arrived. His daughter ended up with over $15,000 in scholarships. He called me and apologized for doubting the process. I told him there was nothing to apologize for. Doubt is natural. Faith is what keeps you going when doubt shows up.

Over the years, I saw repeated confirmation of what I'd read that night. Millions of dollars truly do go unclaimed each year. Not because students are incapable, but because they don't know where to look or they give up before the breakthrough comes.

One national scholarship received fewer than one hundred applications even though it was worth $10,000 and open to students nationwide. The eligibility requirements were straightforward. The essay prompt was clear. But the scholarship required three recommendation letters and a community service portfolio. Most students saw those requirements and moved on to easier applications.

I helped a student named James apply for that scholarship. We worked together to gather his recommendation letters and organize his community service documentation. It took time, but we completed everything thoroughly. He won. That $10,000 changed his life. It covered his first year of college entirely.

James taught me that the scholarships requiring the most effort often have the least competition. Students want quick and easy. They want to submit a simple form and be done. But the scholarships that require thought, effort, and multiple components are often the ones worth pursuing because fewer people complete them.

Now, when I teach parents and students about scholarships, I tell them to treat every opportunity as a blessing waiting to be claimed. Even if the odds seem small, apply anyway. Even if the essay feels intimidating, write it anyway. Yahuah has a way of taking what looks insignificant and turning it into provision.

I also teach them to look for scholarships tied to unique characteristics or circumstances. Scholarships exist for students who are left-handed. For students whose parents work in specific industries. For students with certain last names. For students from particular towns or regions. For students who plan to study obscure subjects.

These niche scholarships often go unclaimed because students don't know they exist or assume they're too specific. But if you fit the criteria, your odds of winning are extremely high because the applicant pool is so small.

One student I worked with discovered a scholarship for students whose parents worked in the railroad industry. His father was a train conductor. The scholarship was worth $5,000 and renewable for four years. He was one of only twelve applicants nationwide. He won and received $20,000 total over his college career.

Another student found a scholarship for students with the last name Johnson who planned to study education. Her last name was Johnson, and she wanted to be a teacher. She applied. She was the only applicant. She received $3,000.

These stories sound almost too good to be true, but they're real. The scholarships are out there. You just have to be willing to look beyond the obvious places.

I also encourage students to apply for scholarships even when they're not a perfect match for the criteria. Some scholarship descriptions say they prefer students with a certain GPA or test score or area of study. Prefer doesn't mean require. If you meet most of the criteria, apply anyway. The worst they can say is no. And sometimes you'll be surprised.

Laura applied for a scholarship that said they preferred students with a 3.8 GPA or higher. Her GPA was 3.6. I told her to apply anyway and use her essay to highlight her other strengths. She wrote about her leadership, her consistency, and her work ethic. She won. The committee told her that while her GPA was slightly below their preference, her overall application demonstrated the character and determination they valued.

That experience taught us not to disqualify ourselves before the committee has a chance to review our application. Let them decide. Your job is to put your best foot forward and trust the process.

The scholarships aren't lost. They're waiting. Waiting for someone prepared enough to apply, persistent enough to follow through, and faithful enough to believe that what's meant for them won't pass them by.

I think about all the students who never discover these opportunities. I think about the families drowning in debt when funding was available all along. It breaks my heart. That's why I'm so passionate about spreading this message. The money is there. You just have to be willing to search for it, apply for it, and believe that you deserve it.

Every time I hear about a student graduating with overwhelming debt, I wonder if they knew about the scholarships that went unclaimed in their field, their region, or their demographic. I wonder if they gave up too soon or never started at all because they assumed scholarships were for someone else.

That's why I tell every family the same thing. Don't assume scholarships aren't for you. Don't assume you won't win.

Don't assume the effort isn't worth it. Apply. Keep applying. And trust that Yahuah will open the right doors at the right time.

### *From the Author's Voice:*

*"Millions in scholarships go unclaimed every year. Don't let your child's blessing sit on someone's desk because you gave up too soon."*

***

# CHAPTER 8: THE FAMILIES I HELPED

*When Faith Turns Blessings Into Ministry*

By the time I realized this journey was bigger than my own household, the evidence was already standing in front of me. One family at a time. One phone call at a time. One breakthrough after another. What started as personal obedience had become shared testimony.

One of the families who applied the information I shared was my dear friend Moncy and her two kids, Isaiah and Kennedy. They happened to be visiting one day while I was preparing for a scholarship presentation I was scheduled to give in Mississippi. I asked if they would mind listening and offering feedback. When I finished, Moncy was blown away by the material I had shared.

We had a conversation and discovered that Isaiah and Kennedy qualified for the Hazelwood Act, a Texas benefit that allows eligible veterans, their spouses, and dependent children to attend public colleges and universities in Texas tuition-free. Simply because their dad had served the military in the state of Texas.

Moncy began to research and confirmed that Isaiah did indeed qualify for the Hazelwood Act. When Isaiah attended college, because of the information I shared with him, he started applying for scholarships. Moncy told me that he received three scholarships his freshman year. And when Kennedy got ready to go off to college, she did the same thing for her.

That presentation in my living room changed the trajectory for both of her children. They not only had tuition covered through the Hazelwood Act, but Isaiah earned additional scholarship money to help with books, housing, and other expenses. Kennedy followed in her brother's footsteps, combining the Hazelwood benefits with scholarships to make her college experience fully funded.

Watching Moncy take what I shared and turn it into provision for her children reminded me that information has power. Sometimes families are just one conversation away from discovering benefits they never knew existed. Sometimes all it takes is someone willing to share what they've learned.

National data helps set realistic expectations for scholarship success. According to Sallie Mae's *How America Pays for College* report, students who receive scholarship and grant aid typically receive between $7,500 and $8,000 per year in combined awards. Most individual scholarship awards are under $2,500, with 97% of scholarship recipients receiving awards in this range. Full-ride scholarships covering all college costs represent less than 0.1% of awarded scholarships. Success comes from stacking numerous smaller scholarships over four years, not from winning one large award. This is exactly how most families successfully fund college through scholarships: consistent effort over time, applying for multiple opportunities, and allowing smaller awards to add up to significant totals.

Moncy's story became one I shared often. When other parents doubted whether scholarships were available, I told them about Isaiah and Kennedy. When families felt overwhelmed by the process, I reminded them that one piece of information can change everything. Their success was proof that awareness combined with action produces results.

I also helped students through church and community programs. Some were first-generation college students who believed scholarships were for other people, not them. Others were discouraged by past rejections or late starts. One young man told me quietly, "Ms. Abbie, I didn't think people like me got scholarships."

I looked him in the eye and said, "People like you are exactly who scholarships are for."

His name was David. He came to one of my workshops at church. He sat in the back row with his arms crossed, looking skeptical. When I asked if anyone had questions, he raised his hand and said, "This might work for some people, but it won't work for me."

I asked him why. He said his grades weren't great. He wasn't in a lot of clubs. He didn't have money for application fees.

He assumed scholarships were for students who had it all together. Students who weren't like him.

I asked him to stay after the workshop so we could talk. Then I asked him about his life. He worked twenty hours a week at a fast-food restaurant to help his single mother pay bills. He took care of his two younger siblings after school. He cooked dinner most nights. He helped them with their homework. He'd been doing this since he was fourteen years old.

I told him that his story was powerful. I told him that responsibility, sacrifice, and perseverance are exactly what scholarship committees look for. He didn't believe me at first. But I convinced him to try.

We worked together for several months. He applied for scholarships focused on first-generation students, students from low-income families, and students who demonstrated resilience. He wrote essays about his life, his responsibilities, and his dreams. He wrote about wanting to become a social worker so he could help families like his own.

Months later, he earned a leadership and perseverance award that covered his first year of tuition. The disbelief on his face when he told me was something I'll never forget.

David called me from the parking lot of his school. He'd just received the letter. He said, "Ms. Abbie, I won. I actually won." His voice shook with excitement and gratitude. I told him I was proud of him. He said, "Nobody has ever been proud of me before." That broke my heart and filled it at the same time.

David went on to attend community college and then transferred to a four-year university. He graduated with a degree in social work. Today, he works with at-risk youth in our community. He tells his story to the young people he mentors, reminding them that scholarships aren't just for perfect students. They're for students who work hard, overcome obstacles, and refuse to give up.

I also worked with a young woman named Tasha, who had a completely different challenge. She had excellent grades and strong test scores, but she had no idea what she wanted to study. Every scholarship application asked about her intended major and career goals, and she didn't have answers. She felt stuck.

I told her it was okay not to have everything figured out. Many students don't know what they want to study when they start college. What mattered was that she could articulate her interests and values. We talked about what she enjoyed. She loved solving problems. She liked working with her hands. She was good at math and science.

We crafted essays that focused on her curiosity and her desire to explore different fields. She wrote about wanting to discover where her skills and passions intersected. She applied for scholarships that valued academic excellence and intellectual curiosity rather than specific career paths. She won several awards totaling over $8,000.

Tasha taught me that you don't need to have your entire life figured out to win scholarships. You just need to be honest about where you are and where you hope to go.

Another student I mentored was dealing with a completely different issue. His name was Kevin, and he'd been homeschooled his entire life. He was worried that scholarship committees wouldn't take him seriously because he didn't attend a traditional high school. He didn't have a class rank. He didn't have the same extracurricular activities as other students.

I told him that homeschooling wasn't a disadvantage. It was just different. We focused on what made his experience unique. He'd taken college courses during his homeschool education. He'd worked on independent research projects. He'd volunteered extensively in the community. His education had been self-directed and rigorous.

We highlighted those strengths in his applications. He wrote about the discipline and time management skills he developed through homeschooling. He wrote about the freedom to pursue his interests deeply rather than broadly. Scholarship committees were impressed. He received over $11,000 in awards.

Kevin's success reminded me that there's no single path to scholarship success. Traditional students can win. Non-traditional students can win. Homeschoolers can win. Students with learning disabilities can win. Students who work full-time can win. The key is telling your story authentically and finding scholarships that value what you bring to the table.

Each family was different. Each story was unique. But the pattern never changed. David's perseverance. Tasha's honesty. Kevin's determination. Different stories, same result, when you do the work, provision follows.

These families are my proof. Not because I did something extraordinary, but because they were willing to do the work and trust the process. Their stories confirm what I now know to be true. This isn't reserved for a few. This is possible for many.

Helping these families changed me. It confirmed my calling. And it showed me that when Yahuah gives you a strategy, it's never meant to stop with you.

Every time I help a family secure scholarships, I think back to sitting at my kitchen table, overwhelmed and unsure, praying for Yahuah to show me the way. He answered that prayer. He gave me a strategy. He opened doors for my daughters. And then He used that experience to help others.

Yahuah blesses you so you can be a blessing. He teaches you so you can teach others. He provides for you so you can help provide for someone else. What He did for my family was never meant to stop with my family. It was always meant to multiply.

They all started in the same place. Overwhelmed. Worried. Unsure. But they all made the same decision. They decided to try. They decided to trust. They decided to do the work even when they didn't know if it would pay off.

And every single one of them saw results. Not because they were smarter or more talented than anyone else, but because they showed up. They stayed consistent. They didn't quit when things got hard. They trusted Yahuah to honor their efforts. And He did.

### *From the Author's Voice:*

*"Every family I've helped is proof that this process works. Your family's testimony is next."*

***

# CHAPTER 9: CHOOSING WISELY: SCHOOL, MAJOR, AND FIT

*Making Strategic Decisions That Honor Yahuah and Secure Your Future*

After helping families secure scholarships, I realized that funding was only part of the equation. The decisions families made about which school to attend, what major to choose, and how far from home to go were just as important as finding the money. A scholarship that covers tuition at the wrong school or for the wrong major can still lead to debt, disappointment, and wasted time.

I've watched too many students make choices based on emotion rather than strategy. They fall in love with the campus. They chase a prestigious name. They follow a dream without counting the cost. Too often, those decisions lead to students coming back home without a degree, buried in debt, and unsure what went wrong.

This chapter is about making wise choices. Choices that honor both your calling and your finances. Choices that set your child up for success, not struggle.

## Understanding Test Scores and School Types

One of the most confusing parts of the college admissions process for families is standardized testing. Parents ask me all the time: how high do the scores need to be? Do test scores really matter? And why do different schools seem to play by different rules?

The truth is this. ACT and SAT scores still matter, just not in the same way they used to. How much they matter depends on the type of institution. They remain important for scholarships, competitive schools, and standing out in large applicant pools.

Understanding the difference between predominantly White Institutions and Historically Black Colleges and Universities can change how you prepare, where you apply, and how much money your child can earn in scholarships.

At many PWIs, especially large public universities and competitive private schools, test scores play a significant role in admissions and scholarships. Average SAT scores for admitted students often fall between 1200 and 1400. ACT scores typically range from 25 to 32. These scores are often tied directly to merit-based scholarships.

For example, a student with a 1300 SAT or a 28 ACT might receive a merit scholarship ranging from $5,000 to $15,000 per year at a PWI. At some schools, scores above that threshold can lead to full tuition or near-full tuition awards, especially when combined with strong grades.

I worked with a student named Michael who had a 1350 SAT score and a 3.8 GPA. He applied to several large state universities. Three of them offered him merit scholarships ranging from $10,000 to $12,000 per year based primarily on his test scores and grades.

But here's the trade-off. Tuition at many PWIs is high. In-state public universities may cost $20,000 to $30,000 per year. Out-of-state or private institutions can exceed $40,000 to $60,000 per year. Even with merit aid, families often face large gaps that lead to student loans.

Michael chose an out-of-state public university that offered him $12,000 per year in merit aid. The total cost of attendance was $45,000 per year. Even with the scholarship, his family had to cover $33,000 annually. They took out loans to cover the difference. By the time he graduated, he had over $60,000 in student debt.

HBCUs evaluate students more holistically. Test scores matter, but they're not the sole focus. Many HBCUs admit students with SAT scores starting around 900 to 1100 or ACT scores between 17 and 23. Strong grades, leadership, recommendations, and personal essays carry significant weight.

This doesn't mean standards are lower. It means standards are broader. HBCUs understand that test scores don't tell the whole story. A student with an SAT score of 1000 might have overcome significant obstacles, worked full-time while attending school, or attended under-resourced schools. HBCUs look at the whole picture.

What many families don't realize is that HBCUs often use test scores strategically to award scholarships. A student with a 1100 SAT or a 22 ACT may receive a scholarship covering $5,000 to $10,000 per year. Scores in the 1200 range can unlock awards that cover full tuition or more.

Both of my daughters attended Tuskegee University, an HBCU. Alayna had an SAT score of 1150 and a GPA of 4.2. Laura had an SAT score of 1100 and a GPA of 4.3. At many PWIs, those scores would've qualified them for modest merit aid at best. At Tuskegee, those scores combined with their leadership and service made them competitive for significant institutional scholarships.

HBCUs also tend to have lower tuition costs. Many HBCUs charge between $15,000 and $20,000 per year for tuition and fees. When combined with institutional scholarships, federal aid, and outside scholarships, the remaining cost can be minimal or even zero.

Another important difference is how scholarships are stacked. At many PWIs, merit aid may reduce need-based aid. At HBCUs, schools are often more flexible. Test score scholarships can stack with departmental awards, alumni scholarships, and private scholarships.

Here's what you need to understand clearly. You don't need a perfect ACT or SAT score to earn scholarship money. You need a strategic score. That means knowing the scholarship cutoffs at the schools you're targeting. It means retaking the test if a few points can move you into a higher scholarship tier. It means choosing schools where your scores work for you, not against you.

Test scores aren't a measure of your child's worth. They're tools. When you understand how that tool works, you can use it to open doors instead of feeling locked out.

## Choosing the Right School

The right school isn't always the most popular or the most impressive-sounding. It's the school that fits your academic profile, your financial situation, and your long-term goals.

Families should ask hard questions before committing. What's the total cost of attendance, not just tuition? How much aid is guaranteed each year? Are scholarships renewable? What percentage of students graduate in four years? How many students transfer out because of cost?

I counseled a family whose daughter was accepted to her dream school, a private university with a strong reputation. The school offered her $10,000 per year in merit aid. The family was excited until we calculated the actual cost. Total cost of attendance was $60,000 per year. Even with the scholarship, they'd need to cover $50,000 annually. Over four years, that meant $200,000.

The family didn't have that kind of money. They'd have to borrow most of it. I asked them if they understood what that debt would mean for their daughter after graduation. Monthly loan payments of over $2,000. Payments that could last for twenty years or more. Payments that would limit where she could live, what job she could take, and when she could start building her own life.

They decided to reconsider. Their daughter ended up attending a state university where the total cost was much lower, and her scholarships covered most of it. She graduated with less than $10,000 in debt, which she paid off within two years of starting her job. She's now thriving, debt-free, and grateful her parents helped her make a wise choice instead of an emotional one.

I always tell parents and students to look at the net price, not the sticker price. A private school with strong scholarships may cost less than a public school with limited aid.

Understanding the difference between sticker price and net price is essential for making informed college decisions. The sticker price is the published cost of attendance, while the net price is what a family actually pays after scholarships, grants, and other aid are applied. According to Federal Student Aid guidelines, total cost of attendance includes not just tuition and fees, but also room and board, books and supplies, transportation, and personal expenses. Many families are surprised to learn that a private school with a high sticker price but generous aid packages may actually cost less than a public university with a lower published price but limited financial assistance.

One student I worked with was choosing between two schools. One was an out-of-state public university that everyone had heard of. The other was an in-state private college. The out-of-state school offered him $5,000 per year. The in-state school offered him $20,000 per year. When we calculated the net cost, the private school was actually $15,000 cheaper per year. He chose the private school and graduated debt-free.

## Choosing the Right Major

Too many students pick majors based on interest alone. Passion matters, but it can't be the only factor. A major must also lead to employability and income that supports independence.

When my daughters started applying to colleges, we talked about more than just where they'd go. We talked about what they wanted to do. I told them, "Your major is more than a subject, it's a direction for your life." Choosing the right path meant finding a balance between passion and practicality.

Alayna always had an analytical mind. She loved science, structure, and solving problems. When she decided to study engineering, it made perfect sense. I encouraged her to pray about it and to make sure it was something she could see herself enjoying long-term. Engineering wasn't only a field she loved but one that offered strong career opportunities. I reminded her that Yahuah gives each of us gifts for a reason, and when we use them wisely, He opens doors that align with both our purpose and our provision.

Laura's path was a little different. She had a natural gift with numbers and a calm, steady personality that made her excellent at managing details. She decided to major in accounting, and it fit her perfectly. One evening, as Laura sat working on her assignments, she paused and shared her thoughts about the future. She told me she wanted a career that allowed her to grow, make an impact, and create stability for herself. Hearing that made me smile. It showed a maturity and clarity that went beyond choosing a major. It revealed that she understood the value of purpose and responsibility, even at a young age.

I've seen students choose majors only because they sound exciting or popular, but years later, they struggle to find work or pay back loans. I always tell parents and students, "Dream big, but plan smart." A fulfilling career is one that uses your gifts while also providing stability. There's nothing wrong with choosing a path that pays well if it allows you to live in purpose and generosity.

Another key part of this process is research. Before choosing a major, we looked at employment trends, salary ranges, and the long-term demand for different professions. I wanted my daughters to understand that college isn't just an experience, it's an investment. You have to think about the return.

National employment data shows that major choice significantly impacts career outcomes. Engineering and other STEM fields have the highest early-career employment rates and starting salaries, often beginning in the $60,000 to $70,000 range or higher. Business and accounting graduates typically start between $45,000 and $55,000. Education and some service fields often start in the $35,000 to $45,000 range. These differences add up over a lifetime of earnings. Understanding these realities helps students make informed choices about balancing passion with financial stability.

I mentored a young man who wanted to major in philosophy. He loved deep thinking and debate. I asked him what jobs he could get with a philosophy degree. He said he hadn't thought about it. We researched together. The career paths were limited. Teaching. Law school. Graduate school. None of those were guaranteed, and most required additional expensive education.

I didn't tell him not to major in philosophy. I told him to think strategically. He ended up double-majoring in philosophy and economics. That combination gave him the intellectual stimulation he craved while also providing marketable skills. He now works in consulting and uses both his philosophical reasoning and economic analysis daily.

This doesn't mean students should abandon their interests. It means they should align their interests with strategy. A student who loves writing might explore communications, technical writing, or marketing. A student who loves helping people might look at healthcare administration, counseling with a plan for licensure, or social services paired with a business minor.

The best outcomes happen when school choice and major choice work together. An affordable school combined with a marketable major creates freedom. Freedom to graduate on time. Freedom to live independently. Freedom to give back instead of struggling to catch up.

But even with all our planning and prayer, there was still a moment of uncertainty. Laura came home from school one day in her junior year and said, "Mama, I don't know if accounting is what I really want to do. It feels boring."

I sat down with her at the kitchen table. "Tell me what you love about numbers," I said.

She thought for a moment, staring at her hands. "I love that they always make sense. I love figuring out problems and finding the answer. Everything balances. Everything has a place."

I smiled. "That's not boring, baby. That's strategy. And the world needs people who can think like that. People who can see the whole picture and make things work."

She looked up at me. "But what if I'm choosing it just because it's safe?"

"Is it safe, or is it wise?" I asked. "There's a difference. Safe means you're afraid. Wise means you're being thoughtful about your future. You're good with numbers. You're organized. You're steady. Those are gifts Yahuah gave you. Using them isn't settling. It's stewardship."

We prayed about it that night. I asked Yahuah to give Laura clarity and peace about her path. I prayed that if accounting wasn't the right choice, He would close that door and open another one. But if it was right, I asked Him to give her confidence and vision for how she could use that degree to serve others and build a stable future.

A few weeks later, she came back to me. "I'm sticking with accounting," she said. "I can see how it fits now. It's not just about balancing spreadsheets. It's about helping people and businesses make good decisions. I can do that."

That conversation taught me something important. Doubt isn't always a sign you're on the wrong path. Sometimes it's just part of the journey. The key is bringing those doubts to Yahuah and letting Him confirm or redirect.

That's the difference between choosing a major because it sounds good and choosing one because it aligns with who Yahuah made you to be. One is based on what impresses other people. The other is based on truth, purpose, and peace.

Today, both of my daughters are thriving in their careers. Alayna's work in engineering has allowed her to travel, grow, and use her skills in meaningful ways. Laura's background in accounting has given her the tools to lead, manage, and plan for her future, and she's now working for one of the top four accounting firms in the country.

Both are now established in their fields, which confirms that the work we put into choosing the right major was worth every conversation.

I also tell families to think about debt when choosing a major. If you're going to borrow money for your education, you need to make sure your future income will allow you to pay it back comfortably. A student who borrows $100,000 to become a teacher will struggle financially for years. But a student who borrows the same amount to become a doctor or engineer will likely be able to manage that debt.

I'm not saying students should only pursue high-paying careers. I'm saying they need to be realistic about debt and income. If you want to be a teacher, find ways to minimize your borrowing. Attend community college first. Go to a state school. Apply for scholarships, live at home. Do whatever it takes to keep your debt low so you can afford to follow your calling.

## Distance From Home

One of the biggest decisions families face when choosing a college is distance. Should your child stay close to home or go far away? There's no universal right answer. There's only the right answer for your child, your family, and your finances.

Many students believe going far away means freedom, growth, and independence. Sometimes that's true. A new environment can build confidence, maturity, and resilience. But distance comes with costs. Out-of-state tuition is often significantly higher. Travel expenses add up quickly. Flights, gas, housing deposits, and emergency trips home can strain a family budget.

I worked with a family whose son wanted to attend school twelve hours away from home. The school was out-of-state, and the tuition reflected that. When we calculated the real cost, including travel expenses, the total was close to $50,000 per year. Even with scholarships, they'd need to borrow a significant amount.

I asked them to consider what would happen if there was an emergency. What if their son got sick and needed to come home immediately? What if there was a family emergency? Those unplanned trips would add even more cost and stress.

The family decided to look at schools closer to home. Their son ended up attending a university two hours away. Close enough to come home when needed, but far enough to have his own college experience. The in-state tuition saved them thousands of dollars per year.

Staying close to home offers different benefits. Lower living costs. Less travel expenses. Stronger family support. Some students perform better when they know help is nearby. Others save thousands by living at home for the first year or two while completing core courses.

I remind families that independence isn't defined by miles. It's defined by responsibility. A student can grow just as much ten minutes from home as ten hours away if expectations are clear and accountability is strong.

Both of my daughters attended Tuskegee University, which was about eleven hours from our home in Katy, Texas. While that was a significant distance from us, it was only three hours away from their grandparents, uncles, and aunts. That proximity to extended family was intentional. Close enough that family could visit occasionally or help if needed without excessive cost. Far enough that they had their own college experience and learned to manage their lives independently.

There were times when that proximity to family mattered. When Alayna got sick during her sophomore year, her Aunt

Terry was able to drive to campus and check on her. That convenience was valuable and saved us money and stress.

Many local and regional scholarships favor students who stay in-state. Some schools offer strong financial incentives for residents. Distance should never cost more than the education is worth.

I counseled a young woman who was torn between two schools. One was across the country and had been her dream school since middle school. The other was in our state. When we compared the financial packages, the difference was staggering. The out-of-state dream school offered her $8,000 per year. The in-state school offered her $18,000 per year, plus state grants. The financial gap was over $14,000 per year - $56,000 over four years.

I asked her if the experience of going far away was worth $56,000 in additional debt. She thought about it for a long time. Eventually, she chose the in-state school. She lived on campus, joined clubs, made friends, and had a full college experience. She graduated debt-free. A few years later, she told me it was the best decision she ever made.

Faith must guide this decision. I encourage parents and students to pray together about location. Ask Yahuah for clarity, not just excitement. Ask for peace, not pressure. The right choice will feel aligned, not forced.

I've seen students choose distant schools they couldn't afford and return home discouraged after one year. I've also seen students stay close, graduate debt-free, and later move anywhere they wanted with freedom and confidence. The difference wasn't ambition. It was planning.

## Making Wise Choices

College is a tool. When used correctly, it builds a life. When used without planning, it can become a burden. The goal isn't just to attend college. The goal is to finish strong, earn wisely, and step into adulthood prepared.

When families approach college with wisdom, planning, and honesty, the results change. Students graduate with confidence instead of fear. Parents breathe easier. Futures look stable instead of uncertain.

I remind families often that finishing matters more than starting. A degree earned from a school you can afford is far more powerful than dropping out of a school you can't. A major that pays the bills creates options. Options reduce stress. Stress reduction leads to better decisions.

Choose the school that fits your financial reality. Choose the major that aligns with your gifts and the job market. Choose the distance that makes sense for your family. And above all, invite Yahuah into every decision. When you do, He will guide you to the right place at the right time for the right reasons.

### *From the Author's Voice:*

*"The right school isn't the one with the best name, it's the one you can afford that leads to the career Yahuah designed you for. Choose with both your head and your heart."*

***

# PART III: FROM BLESSING TO LEGACY

# CHAPTER 10: PURPOSE AND PROVISION

*Choosing a Path That Honors Yahuah and Secures Your Future*

When my daughters started applying to colleges, we talked about more than just where they'd go. We talked about what they wanted to do. I told them, "Your major is more than a subject, it's a direction for your life." Choosing the right path meant finding a balance between passion and practicality.

I remember a conversation I had with Alayna about her future. She would sit at the kitchen table with college brochures spread in front of her, comparing engineering programs. She was drawn to the challenge of the coursework and the problem-solving aspect of the field. But she also had questions. Would she be able to handle the rigor? Would she be one of the few women in her classes? Would the investment be worth it?

We talked through each concern. I reminded her that challenges aren't obstacles. They're opportunities to grow. I told her that being one of the few women in engineering meant she could be a trailblazer for others coming behind her. And yes, the investment would be worth it because engineering degrees lead to stable, well-paying careers that would give her options and freedom.

She prayed about it. We prayed about it as a family. And when she made her final decision, there was peace. That peace confirmed we were on the right path.

Laura had always been the organized one. Even as a child, she kept her room neat and her schoolwork orderly. She liked systems and processes. When we started researching career options, accounting kept coming up as a match for her skills and personality. She wasn't as naturally drawn to it as Alayna was to engineering but she recognized that it was a smart choice.

I told her that sometimes passion grows out of competence. When you're good at something and it provides value to others, you begin to love it. Laura trusted that wisdom. She chose accounting not because it made her heart race with excitement, but because it made sense. It matched her strengths, offered stability and opened doors.

And she was right to trust that process. Today, she loves her work. She's found fulfillment in a field that once felt like just a practical choice.

As they both settled into their programs at Tuskegee University, I watched Yahuah's plan unfold. Their choices weren't random. They were strategic. Both of their degrees carried strong career potential, and both reflected their natural strengths. That balance between calling and opportunity is what I teach every family now.

I've seen students choose majors only because they sound exciting or popular, but years later, they struggle to find work or pay back loans. That's why choosing a major isn't just a personal decision. It's a financial one too.

One young woman I counseled wanted to major in art history. She loved art and could talk for hours about different periods and styles. But when I asked her what jobs were available in that field, she didn't have a clear answer. I wasn't trying to discourage her passion. I was trying to help her think practically about her future.

We researched together. We looked at career paths for art history majors. Museum curator. Art teacher. Gallery manager. Appraiser. The positions existed, but they were limited and often required advanced degrees. The starting salaries were modest. I asked her if she was prepared for that reality. She said she hadn't thought about it.

I encouraged her to consider related fields that offered more career options. Arts administration. Marketing for cultural organizations. Graphic design. She could still be involved in the art world while building a career with more financial stability. She ended up double-majoring in art history and business administration. That combination gave her the knowledge she loved and the skills employers valued. Today, she works in marketing for a major museum. She gets to be immersed in art every day while earning a salary that allows her to live comfortably.

That's the balance I encourage students to find. Follow your interests but also consider the practical realities of the job market.

Choosing wisely means looking beyond your immediate interests to consider long-term sustainability. What seems exciting at eighteen may not sustain you at thirty-five when you have a family to support and bills to pay.

We spent time on websites like the Bureau of Labor Statistics, looking at job outlooks for different careers. We researched which fields were growing and which were shrinking. We looked at median salaries and what kind of lifestyle those salaries would support. We talked about job satisfaction and work-life balance.

This research wasn't meant to kill their dreams. It was meant to inform their decisions. I wanted them to go into their chosen fields with their eyes wide open, understanding what they were signing up for.

These conversations about money and career aren't meant to crush dreams. They're meant to empower students to pursue their passions in financially sustainable ways.

Yahuah cares about every part of our lives, including our finances and careers. He doesn't just want us to follow our dreams blindly, He wants us to follow His direction wisely. I told my daughters, "Pray about your career the same way you pray about your future spouse. You'll be spending a lot of time with it." That always made them laugh, but they understood the meaning.

Career choice isn't just about what you do for eight hours a day. It affects where you live, how much stress you carry, what kind of lifestyle you can afford, and how much time you have for family and other priorities. It's a major life decision that deserves serious prayer and consideration.

Faith guided every decision we made. When opportunities came that didn't feel right, we turned them down. When the right doors opened, we walked through them with confidence. Over time, I saw that when you honor Yahuah in your decisions, He honors you with peace about where you are.

Alayna received offers from several engineering programs. None of the schools offered more scholarship money than Tuskegee did. But when she visited Tuskegee, something deeper clicked. She felt at home. She could picture herself there. There was also something meaningful about the fact that I'd attended Tuskegee Institute and majored in engineering during the short time I was there before I had to leave. Alayna wanted to honor me by attending and graduating from the college I couldn't finish. We prayed about it, and the peace she felt about Tuskegee was undeniable. We trusted that Yahuah was leading her to Tuskegee for a reason.

That decision proved to be right. The connections she made at Tuskegee, the professors who mentored her, and the opportunities she received all confirmed that she was exactly where she was supposed to be. Her choice to attend Tuskegee eventually led to her earning a PhD Fellowship at

FAMU, opening doors we never could have imagined at the beginning of her journey.

Laura's decision process was different. She didn't want to attend Tuskegee at first. She had her own vision for where she wanted to go. But we had to convince her that it made financial sense. No other school offered more money than Tuskegee did. Beyond the finances, there were practical benefits. She'd have family there with her. She and Alayna could drive back and forth together from school to home, which mattered because we only had one car for them to share. As a freshman, Laura couldn't have a car on campus at most universities, but Alayna could. Sharing transportation made things easier for both of them. On top of all that, they both received a sibling credit for attending the same college, which saved us even more money.

Once Laura understood the full picture, she agreed. And like Alayna, she came to see that Tuskegee was exactly where she was supposed to be. The family connection mattered to her. I had attended Tuskegee, even though I hadn't finished. Going there meant something to both of us. It felt like coming full circle like Yahuah was redeeming what had been lost.

Today, both of my daughters are thriving in their careers. Alayna's work in engineering has allowed her to travel, grow, and use her skills in meaningful ways. Laura's background in accounting has given her the tools to lead, manage, and plan for her future, and she's now working for one of the top four accounting firms in the country. Watching them succeed in fields that fit their purpose is proof that prayerful planning works.

When Laura got the offer from one of the Big Four accounting firms, she called me with such excitement. She said, "Mama, I made it." I told her I always knew she would. She had worked hard. She had been faithful. She had made smart decisions. Yahuah had honored all of it.

Alayna's career has taken her places we never imagined. She's worked on projects that challenge her and allow her to use her gifts. She's traveled internationally. She's mentored younger engineers. She loves what she does, and that love shows in the quality of her work.

Balancing financial considerations and career goals is really about trust. You do your research, you prepare, and then you leave the outcome in Yahuah's hands. When you move in faith and wisdom, He'll make sure you're positioned exactly where you need to be.

I also tell families to think about debt when choosing a major. If you're going to borrow money for your education, you need to make sure your future income will allow you to pay it back comfortably. A student who borrows $100,000 to become a teacher will struggle financially for years. But a student who borrows the same amount to become a doctor or engineer will likely be able to manage that debt.

I'm not saying students should only pursue high-paying careers. I'm saying they need to be realistic about debt and income. If you want to be a teacher, find ways to minimize your borrowing. Attend community college first. Go to a state school. Apply for scholarships. Live at home. Do whatever it takes to keep your debt low so you can afford to follow your calling.

One young man I counseled wanted to be a youth pastor. He felt called to ministry. But the private Christian college he wanted to attend would've left him with $60,000 in debt. I explained that debt would limit his ability to serve. Churches often don't pay youth pastors high salaries. He'd spend years struggling to pay back loans instead of focusing on his ministry.

We found a different path. He attended community college for two years, then transferred to a state school where he majored in social work with a minor in religious studies. He graduated with minimal debt. Today, he works as a youth pastor and lives comfortably. He is free to serve without the burden of overwhelming financial obligations.

That's the kind of strategic thinking I encourage. Follow your calling but do it wisely. Don't let debt steal your future.

I also remind students that their first job doesn't have to be their forever job. Your major gives you a foundation. Where you go from there is up to you. Alayna may not be an engineer forever. Laura may not stay in accounting her whole career. But the skills they learned, the degrees they earned, and the financial stability they built give them options. That's what education should do. It should open doors, not close them.

Both of my daughters have talked about eventually starting their own businesses. Alayna has ideas for consulting work.

Laura has thought about opening her own firm. Their degrees give them the credibility and knowledge to do that when the time is right.

That's the power of a strategic education. It doesn't lock you into one path. It gives you the tools to create your own path when you're ready.

### *From the Author's Voice:*

*"Purpose and provision go hand in hand. When you honor Yahuah with your plans, He'll align your passion with prosperity and your calling with contentment."*

***

134

# CHAPTER 11: FROM BLESSING TO CALLING

*How Helping Families Find Scholarships Became My Purpose*

Every time I help a family secure a scholarship, it feels just as meaningful as when my own daughters received theirs. Watching hard work turn into breakthrough never gets old. Each success is a reminder that Yahuah's favor is limitless, and that what He does for one, He's willing to do for another.

After my daughters' success, more families began reaching out for guidance. At first, I didn't think much of it. I didn't have a business plan, a program, or a name for what I was doing. I simply shared what had worked for us. Conversations started at my kitchen table, during phone calls, and after church services. Parents asked questions. Students asked for help. And I answered, one conversation at a time.

What I quickly realized was that this was no longer casual advice. Families were carrying the same fear I once carried. They were overwhelmed by deadlines, confused by requirements, and unsure where to begin. When I sat with them, explained the process, and helped them organize their next steps, I watched that fear begin to lift. Confidence replaced panic. Purpose replaced uncertainty.

The first time I realized this work was becoming something bigger was when a coworker approached me during lunch. She'd heard about my daughters' scholarship success and wanted to know if I could help her son. We met after work that same week, and I walked her through the entire process. She took detailed notes, asked thoughtful questions, and left with a plan.

That conversation planted a seed. If one parent needed help, there were probably dozens more who felt the same way. I started paying attention to the conversations happening around me at work, at church, at school events. Everywhere I went, parents were talking about college costs and expressing anxiety about how they would afford them.

I began offering to help. At first, people were hesitant. They didn't want to impose or take up my time. I assured them it wasn't an imposition. It was a joy. Watching families discover what was possible brought me more fulfillment than I could have imagined.

Some families came to me at the beginning of their journey. Others arrived late, believing they'd already missed their chance. In both cases, the results were the same when they stayed committed. When students applied consistently, prepared thoughtfully, and trusted the process, opportunities began to appear. Award letters arrived. Relief followed. And with each success, belief grew stronger.

One mother came to me in January of her son's senior year. Most scholarship deadlines had already passed. She was convinced it was too late. I told her it wasn't. There were still hundreds of scholarships available with deadlines in the spring and summer. Some didn't even have deadlines. They accepted applications year-round.

We got to work immediately. Her son applied for every scholarship we could find that fit his profile. He wrote essays. He gathered recommendation letters. He submitted applications weekly. By the time he graduated in May, he'd secured over $10,000 in scholarships. Not enough to cover everything, but enough to make his first year affordable. His mother called to thank me with such gratitude. She said I'd given her son a chance he wouldn't have had otherwise.

I told her I didn't give him anything. I just showed him where to look. He did the rest.

I also worked with students through church and community programs. Some were first-generation college students who had never seen anyone in their family attend college, let alone pay for it without loans. Others had faced personal setbacks and were convinced scholarships were out of reach. But once they saw what was possible, something shifted. Hope returned. Effort followed.

One young woman came to a workshop I held at church. She sat quietly in the back, barely participating. After the session ended, she lingered. When everyone else had left, she approached me. She said she wanted to go to college but didn't think she was smart enough. Her grades were average.

She wasn't involved in many activities. She assumed scholarships were for students who had more to offer.

I asked her to tell me about herself. She worked part-time at a nursing home, caring for elderly residents. She'd been doing it for two years. She loved the residents and felt called to work in healthcare. She wanted to become a nurse.

I told her that her experience was valuable. Scholarship committees want to support students who have real-world experience and clear career goals. Her work at the nursing home demonstrated compassion, responsibility, and commitment. Those qualities mattered just as much as grades.

We worked together for several months. She applied for scholarships focused on healthcare careers, community service, and students from working families. She wrote essays about her experiences at the nursing home and her desire to care for others. She won multiple scholarships totaling over $8,000.

When she called to tell me, her voice was full of excitement and disbelief. She said no one had ever believed in her before. I told her I was simply helping her see what was already there. The potential had always been inside her. She just needed someone to help her recognize it.

One student told me quietly, "College isn't for people from where I come from." I looked at him and said, "People like you are exactly who scholarships are for. You just have to claim what's already waiting for you." Months later, he earned an award that covered his first year of tuition. That moment reinforced everything I believed about this work.

His name was Antonio, and he came from a rough neighborhood. He'd seen friends drop out of school. He'd seen people give up on their dreams. He didn't want that life, but he didn't know how to get out. College seemed like something for other people. People with money, people with connections. Not people like him.

I told him that wasn't true. College is for anyone willing to work for it. Scholarships are for anyone willing to apply for them. I showed him how to search. I helped him write his essays. I encouraged him when he wanted to quit.

Antonio is now in his third year of college, studying criminal justice. He wants to become a police officer in his community. He wants to be the kind of officer who builds relationships and makes a difference. His story is proof that where you start doesn't determine where you finish.

Over time, I began to see a clear pattern. Every success story was different, but the foundation was the same. The more families I helped, the more obvious it became. This wasn't a coincidence. This was Yahuah honoring what they brought to the table. It wasn't just about money. It was about restoring hope, shifting mindsets, and showing families that Yahuah provides when you trust Him and do your part.

I started keeping a journal of the families I worked with. I wrote down their names, their stories, and their outcomes. Looking back through that journal now, I'm overwhelmed by what Yahuah has done. Hundreds of thousands of dollars in scholarships. Dozens of students attend college debt-free. Families transformed by hope and possibility.

Each entry in that journal represents a life changed. A burden lifted. A future secured. That journal is one of my most treasured possessions because it's a record of Yahuah's faithfulness.

Sometimes I think back to that quiet night at the kitchen table when this journey began. I didn't know then that one small step of faith would grow into something that would touch so many lives. What started as a search to fund my daughters' education became a calling to help others walk the same path with confidence and peace.

I didn't set out to start a business or a ministry. I just wanted to help my daughters. But Yahuah had bigger plans. He used my desperation to birth something that would bless others. He turned my struggle into strategy. He turned my testimony into teaching.

That's how Yahuah works. He wastes nothing. Every challenge you face. Every lesson you learn. Every victory you win. He can use it all to help someone else.

This chapter of the journey taught me that when you share what you've learned, impact multiplies. One family's breakthrough becomes encouragement for another. What begins as obedience in one season can become purpose in the next.

I also learned that this work requires boundaries. In the beginning, I said yes to everyone. I met with families at all hours. I answered calls and texts late into the night. I poured myself out trying to help as many people as possible. Eventually, I realized I was burning out. I couldn't sustain that pace.

I had to learn to set limits. I established office hours. I created group workshops instead of only doing one-on-one sessions. I developed materials families could use on their own. I learned to say no when I needed to rest.

Setting boundaries didn't mean I cared less. It meant I was being a better steward of the gift Yahuah had given me. I couldn't help anyone if I was exhausted and depleted. Taking care of myself allowed me to serve others more effectively.

I also had to accept that not every family would succeed. Some started strong but lost momentum. Some weren't willing to put in the work. Some gave up after a few rejections. I used to take that personally. I felt like I'd failed them.

But I learned that I can't want success for someone more than they want it for themselves. My job is to provide the tools, the knowledge, and the encouragement. Their job is to do the work. I can open the door, but they have to walk through it.

That realization freed me. I stopped carrying guilt for families who didn't follow through. I celebrated the ones who did and trusted that I had planted seeds even with those who quit. Maybe they weren't ready at that moment, but the information was there when they were.

As word spread about the work I was doing, opportunities began to open. Schools and community centers invited me to speak. I started conducting workshops for parents and students. What began as informal conversations at my kitchen table was becoming something more structured and intentional.

In 2015, I officially launched Parent Project LLC. The name represented what the work had always been about. Parents partnering with their children. Families working together toward a shared goal. A project built on faith, preparation, and persistence.

Parent Project LLC became the vehicle through which I could reach more families. I developed a curriculum. I created workbooks. I built a system that families could follow from start to finish. As the work grew, others volunteered to support the speaking engagements and help share the message. The ministry was expanding beyond what I could do alone.

But even as it grew, the heart of the work remained the same. Sitting with families. Listening to their fears. Helping them see possibility where they once saw impossibility. Celebrating with them when award letters arrived. Praying with them when rejections came.

That's the part that still brings me the most joy. The personal connection. The individual stories. The moment when a parent realizes their child can actually go to college, the moment when a student realizes they're worthy of investment.

Those moments never get old. They fuel me. They remind me why I do this work.

Today, I continue this mission through workshops, consultations, and community programs. I speak at churches, schools, and conferences. I mentor parents who want to help their own children. I train counselors and educators who want to better serve their students. The work has expanded, but the mission has remained the same.

Every family I work with carries a piece of my story. They carry the legacy of what Yahuah did for my daughters. They carry the hope that if it works for us, it can work for them too. And when they succeed, they will carry that same message to others.

That's how generational blessings work. They don't stop with you. They multiply. They spread. They create a ripple effect that touches lives you may never meet.

### From the Author's Voice:

*"What Yahuah does for you is never just for you. He blesses you so you can turn around and bless someone else. That's how legacies are born."*

***

# CHAPTER 12: WHEN YAHUAH SHOWS UP

*Trusting Yahuah's Timing in Every Step*

Faith was the foundation of everything we did. Every scholarship, opportunity, and open door reflected Yahuah's grace and timing. Preparation and effort took us far, but faith carried us the rest of the way.

There were times when things didn't go according to plan. Deadlines slipped by. Essays needed rewrites. An expected award didn't come through. Discouragement tried to creep in, but prayer kept us steady. Each time I turned to Yahuah, He reminded me that His timing is always perfect. What felt like a setback was often just a setup for something greater.

I learned to recognize the difference between a closed door and a delayed answer. Sometimes what looks like rejection is actually redirection. Sometimes what feels like a *no* is really a *not yet*. Yahuah sees what we can't see. He knows what we need before we need it. Our job is to trust Him even when we can't trace Him.

This lesson became clearer with every unexpected turn in our journey. There were scholarships we thought were perfect fits that resulted in rejections. There were opportunities we almost missed that turned into significant blessings. There were moments when I questioned whether we were on the right path, only to see Yahuah confirm that we were exactly where we needed to be.

Early in Alayna's senior year, she applied for a scholarship and worked hard on that essay. We both felt confident. Weeks went by with no response. Months passed, and we assumed it wasn't meant to be. We'd moved on. Then one afternoon, a letter arrived from the same organization this time for a different program name. It was a bigger award, renewable every year, with a book stipend included.

"You did it again, Yahuah. You gave us something better than we asked for."

That's the lesson I keep learning. His timing isn't about delay. It's about positioning us for the right blessing at the right time.

That scholarship ended up being worth $16,000 over four years instead of the $5,000 one-time award she'd originally applied for. What we thought was a loss was actually Yahuah positioning her for something better.

That experience taught me to stop mourning closed doors. Every closed door is Yahuah's protection or redirection. He's not withholding good things from us. He's protecting us from the wrong things and positioning us for the right things.

Laura experienced something similar in college. One semester, she faced an unexpected expense that wasn't covered by financial aid. Her accounting textbooks for that term cost $800. More than she'd budgeted. More than we had set aside. I could hear the worry in her voice when she called.

But instead of panicking, instead of asking me to send money we didn't have, she took a breath and said, "Mama, let's pray about it."

We prayed together over the phone. Short. Simple. Honest. "Yahuah, we need $800 for Laura's books. We've done everything we know to do. We trust you to provide."

Two weeks passed. I checked in with Laura every few days. She was calm, focused on her classes, and trusting.

Then I asked Laura to go to the accounting department and ask the staff if they could help in any way. They did. $650. Most people don't know that each department at a university has funding to use at their discretion. And if you're a model student, a student who attends classes, participates on campus, and keeps up good grades, those departments will be willing to help you out whenever you're short on funds. But they have to know who you are. You have to go to those departments and meet the staff, the dean, and network.

That $650 covered most of what she needed, and we were able to manage the rest. That kind of provision is no coincidence. That's Yahuah showing up in the details. That's Him reminding us that He knows what we need before we ask, and He provides exactly what we need exactly when we need it.

"I told you," I said to Laura. "I would always believe it when it comes to Yahuah. He specializes in showing up right on time with exactly what we need."

That's the kind of favor you can't explain, only thank Him for.

Faith guided every decision we made. I didn't always know the next step, but I trusted Yahuah to provide what we needed when the time came. Over and over, he did just that.

There were nights when I lay in bed wondering if I was doing enough. Wondering if I'd missed a scholarship or overlooked an opportunity. Wondering if my daughters would have enough funding when the time came to enroll. In those moments, I had to choose faith over fear. I had to remind myself that Yahuah had brought us this far, and He wouldn't abandon us now.

I prayed the same prayer over and over. "Yahuah, I've done everything I know to do. The rest is up to You. I trust you to provide." That prayer became my anchor. It kept me from spiraling into anxiety. It reminded me that I wasn't in this alone.

Now, when I mentor other families, I can sense that same grace guiding them. Parents often call me anxious and overwhelmed, unsure where to start. I remind them, "You're right on time. Yahuah's favor doesn't operate on human schedules, it operates on obedience."

One mother called me in tears because her daughter's scholarship application had been rejected. She said, "Abbie, we prayed about this. We did everything right. Why didn't she get it?" I told her I didn't know why, but I knew Yahuah had a reason. I encouraged her to keep applying and trust that the right scholarships would come.

Two months later, that same daughter received three scholarship offers in one week, totaling more than the scholarship she'd been rejected for. The mother called me back and said, "You were right. Yahuah knew what He was doing." I told her Yahuah always knows what He's doing. Our job is to trust Him, even when we can't see the full picture.

Favor also brings humility. It reminds us that every win isn't our doing but His. We can plan, organize, and prepare, but only Yahuah can open the right doors. His favor is what turns effort into success, worry into peace, and dreams into testimony.

I've seen favor show up in ways that can't be explained by effort alone. Scholarships awarded to students who weren't the most qualified on paper. Opportunities that came through random conversations or chance encounters. Doors that opened at the last possible moment when all hope seemed lost.

One student I worked with applied for a scholarship that required an interview. She was nervous because public speaking wasn't her strength. We practiced together. We went over potential questions and crafted thoughtful answers. But when the day of the interview arrived, she was still anxious.

She called me afterward and said the interview hadn't gone well. She stumbled over her words. She forgot some of the points she wanted to make. She left feeling defeated. I told her to pray and trust that Yahuah would work it out.

A week later, she received a call letting her know she had been selected. She was shocked and asked how she could have won when she felt she hadn't done well. The committee told her they were impressed by her sincerity and authenticity. They said many candidates gave polished, rehearsed answers, but she was genuine. Her nervousness actually worked in her favor because it showed she cared deeply about the opportunity.

That's favor. That's Yahuah taking what we think is a weakness and turning it into a strength.

Faith and favor go hand in hand. Faith keeps you moving when results seem delayed. Favor shows up when preparation meets divine timing. Together, they transform what looks impossible into a story worth telling.

I've also learned that favor doesn't always look the way we expect. Sometimes favor is getting exactly what you asked for. Other times, favor is not getting what you asked for because Yahuah has something better in mind. Both require trust.

There was a scholarship Alayna wanted desperately. It was prestigious, well-known, and would've looked impressive on her résumé. She spent weeks on the application. She poured her heart into the essay. She submitted everything carefully.

She didn't get it.

She was heartbroken. I was disappointed too. We had prayed specifically for that scholarship. We had believed she would receive it. When the rejection came, it shook her confidence. She wondered if she was good enough. She wondered if all the effort had been a waste.

I told her to trust Yahuah. Rejection isn't a reflection of her worth, it's simply redirection. A few months later, she received a scholarship she hadn't even been focused on. It was worth more money than the one she'd been rejected for, and it came with mentorship opportunities that shaped her career.

Looking back, we both see that the rejection was a blessing. Yahuah knew what she needed even when we didn't.

When I look at my daughters today, I see living proof of that truth. Their success wasn't luck; it was Yahuah's faithfulness. He didn't just bless their education, He used their journey to strengthen our family's faith.

Alayna and Laura are both thriving in their careers now, but they still talk about the scholarship journey. They still remember the late nights, the rejections, the prayers, and the breakthrough moments. They know that what they've accomplished isn't because of their own strength. It's because Yahuah was faithful every step of the way.

That knowledge has shaped how they approach challenges now. When things don't go as planned, they don't panic. They pray. When doors close, they look for where Yahuah is opening another one. When fear tries to creep in, they remember what Yahuah has already done and trust Him to do it again.

Faith has also shaped how they steward their blessings. Both of my daughters are generous. They give back to their communities. They mentor younger students. They support causes they believe in. They understand that what Yahuah gave them wasn't just for them. It was so they could be a blessing to others.

They are living proof that when Yahuah blesses you, He does it so you can turn around and bless others. Their success isn't just about them. It's about the students they'll inspire, the families they'll encourage, and the legacy they'll leave.

I've also learned that favor isn't always immediate. Sometimes Yahuah's favor shows up years later in ways you never expected. Doors open because of relationships you built during the scholarship process. Opportunities come because of the discipline and work ethic you developed while applying. Skills you learned while writing essays serve you later in your career.

The scholarship journey was never just about getting money for college. It was about building character. Developing perseverance. Strengthening faith. Learning to trust Yahuah in the waiting. Those lessons are worth more than any scholarship.

When I speak to families now, I tell them to keep that perspective. Yes, the goal is to secure funding for college. But the process itself is shaping your child into the person they need to become. Rejections teach resilience. Waiting teaches patience. Breakthroughs teach gratitude. All of it matters.

I also remind families that Yahuah's favor isn't limited to scholarships. His favor extends to every area of life. The same faith that helps you trust Him for scholarships will help you trust Him for healing, provision, relationships, and purpose. This journey is a training ground for a lifetime of walking by faith.

Looking back, I see Yahuah's hand in every part of our journey. The timing of every scholarship. The connections we made. The lessons we learned. The doors that opened. The doors that closed. All of it was orchestrated by Him.

I didn't always see it at the moment. There were times when I was frustrated or confused. Times when I questioned why things weren't working out the way I thought they should. But with the benefit of hindsight, I see that Yahuah was working everything together for our good. He was writing a story bigger than what I could see at the time.

That's the nature of faith. It requires us to trust what we can't see. To believe that Yahuah is working even when we can't trace His hand. To keep moving forward even when the path isn't clear.

And when we do that, when we choose faith over fear and trust over doubt, we position ourselves to see His favor in ways that leave us in awe. We get to witness miracles. We get to see impossible situations turn into testimonies. We get to experience the goodness of Yahuah in ways that go beyond what we could ask or imagine.

*From the Author's Voice:*

"Yahuah's timing is perfect, even when it feels late. Every 'no' is protecting you from the wrong thing. Every 'yes' arrives exactly when it's meant to."

***

# CHAPTER 13: BUILDING A LEGACY

---◆---

*Turning One Family's Journey Into a Mission for Many*

What began as a personal mission grew into a legacy of learning, service, and giving. My original goal was simple: to help my daughters go to college without debt. I didn't realize that Yahuah was shaping something much bigger, a purpose that would continue long after they graduated.

A legacy isn't measured by money or titles. It's defined by the values you pass on, the lives you touch, and the light you leave behind. Through this journey, I discovered that education is one of the most powerful gifts you can give to your family and community.

After Alayna and Laura graduated, our family made a commitment to keep helping others. We knew the struggle, the searching, and the prayers it took to find resources, and we wanted to make that road easier for other families. What began around our kitchen table turned into a ministry rooted in purpose and impact.

The decision to continue this work after my daughters graduated was intentional. I could have stopped. I could have said my job was done and moved on to other things. But I knew that what Yahuah had given me wasn't just for my household.

My daughters were on board from the beginning. They understood that their success story could inspire others. They were willing to share their experiences, speak at workshops, and encourage younger students. They saw themselves as living proof that the process works, and they wanted others to benefit from what we had learned.

Over time, helping students find scholarships became more than advice, it became a calling. I saw how one family's breakthrough could inspire an entire community. Parents who once felt defeated found hope again. Students who doubted themselves began to believe in what was possible.

At one workshop I hosted at church, more than fifty people showed up. Parents filled every seat. Some brought their children. Some brought notebooks and highlighted printouts of scholarship information. The energy in that room was electric. People were hungry for answers. They were tired of feeling helpless about college costs. They wanted solutions.

I shared our story that day. I walked them through the process step by step. I showed them the binder system. I gave them website lists. I answered questions for more than hours. When the workshop ended, people lined up to thank me. One mother hugged me and said, "You just gave me hope."

That moment confirmed what I already knew. This work wasn't just about scholarships. It was about restoring belief. Belief that college is possible. Belief that debt isn't inevitable. Belief that Yahuah provides when you do your part.

I also watched my daughters embrace the same heart for service. Alayna loves giving back to the community and tutors students in math and science. One of her students learned about the work I do helping families find scholarships, and his parents reached out for help. I had the privilege of mentoring him through the college admissions process and helping him secure scholarships to attend the school of his dreams. Seeing Alayna's example inspire others reminded me that legacy multiplies when you lead by example.

That young man's name was Jordan. He was a quiet kid with a lot of potential but not much confidence. Alayna had been tutoring him in calculus, and over time, they developed a mentor-mentee relationship. He trusted her. When she told him about the scholarship work I did, he was skeptical. He said scholarships were for smart kids, and he didn't see himself that way.

Alayna told him that wasn't true. She told him about her own journey and how scholarships weren't just about grades. They were about character, persistence, and telling your story. She encouraged him to talk to me.

Jordan and I met several times over the course of his senior year. We worked on essays. We searched for scholarships. We prayed together. By graduation, he'd received enough funding to attend a state university without taking out loans. He is now studying computer science and thriving.

Jordan's success meant the world to Alayna. She saw that her influence extended beyond tutoring. She was shaping his future by introducing him to possibilities he didn't know existed. That's legacy. That's the impact.

Later, I had the honor of serving on the Houston Tuskegee University Alumni Board, which felt like another full-circle blessing. In that role, I helped raise funds to support students who were struggling to stay in school. Years earlier, I'd been that student, quietly praying for help. Now, Yahuah had placed me in a position to help answer those same prayers for others. It was an incredible honor to pour into young people walking a path I once walked myself.

Serving on that board was emotional for me. Every time we reviewed scholarship applications or discussed students who needed emergency funding, I thought about my younger self. I thought about how different my life might have been if I'd known where to find help. I thought about the dreams I'd had to put on hold because I couldn't afford to stay.

But I also felt deep gratitude. Gratitude that Yahuah had redeemed my story. Gratitude that what was meant to break me had actually prepared me to help others. Gratitude that I could now stand in the gap for students facing the same struggle I once faced.

We raised thousands of dollars through alumni events and campaigns. We awarded scholarships to Houston-area high school seniors who planned to attend Tuskegee, and when funds were available, we also helped current college students stay enrolled. We covered emergency expenses for students facing unexpected financial challenges. Every dollar we raised represented hope for a student who needed it.

One year, we helped a young woman who was a semester away from graduating but couldn't afford to register for her final classes. She owed the school money from a previous semester, and they wouldn't let her enroll until the balance was paid. She was devastated. She'd worked so hard and was so close to finishing.

The alumni board stepped in and covered her balance. She was able to register, complete her degree, and graduate on time. That work reminded me why this mission is so important. It's not just about money. It's about dignity. It's about telling students that they're seen, valued, and worth investing in.

Laura continued to reflect that same spirit of excellence and generosity. During her senior year of high school, she received a Houston Tuskegee Alumni Association Scholarship Award, another reminder that blessings continue to follow obedience.

Laura was grateful for that scholarship, and she understood the responsibility that came with it. She knew someone had invested in her, and she wanted to honor that investment by investing in others. During her time at Tuskegee, she tutored freshmen in accounting and math. She wanted to give back while she was still a student, not wait until years later.

I was grateful for the impact the Houston Tuskegee Alumni Association had on Laura, and I volunteered to work with them to give back. Many students receive scholarships and move on without thinking about who made it possible. But our family thought about it constantly. We wrote thank-you notes to donors. We stayed connected with the alumni association. We looked for ways to serve even while we were still benefiting from the generosity of others.

That spirit of gratitude and reciprocity is what builds lasting legacies. It's what ensures that the cycle of blessing continues from one generation to the next.

Now, I continue that mission as President of the Moss Point High School Class of 1980 Scholarship Committee, where we raise money each year to help students attend college. I oversee fundraising and help select the recipients for our annual awards. It's one of the greatest honors of my life because I understand the challenges students face and the determination it takes to succeed.

Being part of the MPHS Class of 1980 Scholarship Committee brought me full circle in yet another way. Moss Point is where I grew up. It's where my story began. To be able to return and serve students from my hometown feels like a divine assignment.

We host fundraisers once a year. Donation drives during class reunions. Every dollar raised goes directly to scholarships for graduating seniors. We award three $1,000 scholarships each year. Every scholarship matters. Even a $500 award can make the difference between a student enrolling or giving up.

I take the selection process seriously. I read every application carefully. I look for students who remind me of my daughters. Students who are working hard despite challenges. Students who have a clear vision for their future. Students who will use their education to give back.

We also look for students who might not have the highest GPAs or test scores but who demonstrate character, resilience, and determination. Those qualities often matter more than grades. A student with a 3.0 GPA who works twenty hours a week to help their family and still maintains their commitments is just as deserving as a student with a 4.0.

Each year, the MPHS Class of 1980 Scholarship Committee presents our awards during the MPHS Senior Night ceremony. We choose and notify the students before the event. Watching their faces light up never gets old. Seeing parents express relief and gratitude reminds me why I do this work. Each scholarship represents hope, opportunity, and a chance to build a better future.

Then there's the moment I wait for every year. I watch students walk across the stage to receive their awards. Some are surprised. Some are overcome with emotion. Some can't believe their name was called. I see grandparents in the audience wiping their eyes. I see parents recording on their phones. I see younger siblings watching wide-eyed, maybe imagining their own futures.

One year, a young man came up to me afterward. He was holding his scholarship certificate like it was the most precious thing he had ever received. He looked me in the eye and said, "Ms. Huckleby, thank you. My mama didn't think I could go to college. Now she knows I can."

I stood there looking at him, this tall young man with his whole future ahead of him and I felt my eyes fill with emotion. His mama didn't think he could go. Maybe because money was tight. Maybe because no one in their family had gone before. Maybe because the world had told them college was for other people's children, not theirs.

But now she knows he can.

I thought about his mother sitting in that audience, watching her son's name get called. I thought about the shift that happened in her heart at that moment. Hope replacing doubt. Possibility of replacing limitations. Pride replacing fear.

I thought about all the mothers like her. Mothers who work multiple jobs. Mothers who sacrifice daily. Mothers who want better for their children but don't know how to make it happen. Mothers who pray in the quiet hours, asking Yahuah to make a way.

That young man's scholarship was an answer to his mother's prayers. And being part of that answer is the greatest privilege of my life.

That moment reminded me why I do this. It's not just about the money. It's about showing families that their dreams are possible when they prepare and trust Yahuah's plan. It's about changing what a family believes about themselves and their future.

That's legacy. Not what you keep, but what you give away. It's not about how much you accumulate, but how much you contribute. It's about the ripple effect your faith and actions create in the lives of others.

I think about the students I've helped over the years. Many of them have graduated now. Some have gone on to graduate school. Others have started careers. A few have even started families of their own. I wonder how many of them will remember the scholarship process and use what they learned to help their own children. I hope they do. I hope the legacy continues.

Yahuah took one mother's determination and turned it into a generational mission. Every family I help, every scholarship awarded, and every student who crosses that stage is proof of His faithfulness. What started as a personal pursuit became a lifelong purpose to educate, empower, and encourage others to dream bigger and believe deeper.

I also see legacy in the families I've mentored who are now mentoring others. Monica, whose children Caleb and Renee both went to college debt-free, now helps other parents in her community. She shares what she learned. She walks them through the process. She has become an extension of the work Yahuah started in my kitchen.

Legacy multiplies this way. It doesn't stay with one person. It spreads. It reproduces. It creates a network of people committed to helping others succeed.

I've also seen legacy in unexpected places. A parent I helped five years ago recently told me that her daughter, now a college graduate, is using the organizational skills she learned during the scholarship process in her career. She said the binder system we created for scholarships became the foundation for how her daughter manages projects at work.

That kind of legacy goes beyond scholarships. It's about teaching life skills. Teaching discipline. Teaching faith. Teaching young people that hard work and preparation open doors.

Legacy is also about breaking cycles. I broke the cycle of unfinished education in my family. My daughters graduated debt-free and are now thriving in their careers. The families I've helped are breaking cycles of poverty, debt, and limited opportunity. Their children will grow up with different examples and different possibilities.

That's the power of legacy. It doesn't just affect one generation. It affects many. It changes trajectories. It rewrites family stories.

### *From the Author's Voice:*

*"Legacy is built on love, faith, and service. When you give freely and lead with purpose, Yahuah multiplies your impact beyond anything you could ever imagine."*

***

# PART IV: LIVING THE LEGACY

# WHERE ARE THEY NOW?

◆

Today, Alayna works as a Materials Science Engineer at a major Oil & Gas company in Houston, TX. She graduated from Tuskegee University debt-free with her engineering degree, then attended FAMU on a PhD Fellowship in Materials Science Engineering. After completing her graduate work, she stepped into a career that allows her to use her gifts while building financial stability. She's saving and investing toward her first home, travels when she wants, and gives generously to causes she believes in. None of that would've been possible if she'd been burdened with student loan payments.

When I asked her recently what graduating debt-free meant to her, she said, "Mama, it meant freedom. Freedom to choose my first job based on where I wanted to grow, not just where the salary was highest. Freedom to save and invest early. Freedom to help others without feeling stretched thin myself."

Alayna tutors junior and senior high school students in math and science. She tells them her story and encourages them to pursue scholarships with the same determination she did.

She understands that the scholarship journey wasn't just about paying for college. It was about building character, developing discipline, and learning to trust Yahuah's timing.

Laura is a senior tax accountant for a firm in Virginia. Like her sister, she graduated from Tuskegee University debt-free. After undergrad, she earned her master's degree from the university of Houston, then entered the workforce without the weight of student loans. She manages her finances with the same strategic mindset we used during the scholarship process. She budgets intentionally, saves consistently, and gives faithfully.

Laura recently told me, "The best part about not having student loans is that I get to build the life I want now, not ten years from now. I'm not waiting to be debt-free before I start living. I already am."

Both of my daughters are living proof that this process works. They're thriving in their careers, building their futures, and walking in the freedom that comes from wise decisions made early. They're not weighed down by debt. They're not stressed about monthly loan payments. They're not putting off dreams because of financial burdens.

The scholarships we fought for did more than pay for their education. They gave my daughters options. They gave them peace. They gave them the ability to step into adulthood with confidence instead of anxiety.

When I look at them now, I don't just see successful young women. I see the faithfulness of Yahuah. I see the fruit of preparation, persistence, and prayer. I see evidence that when you do your part and trust Him with the rest, He will open doors that no one can close.

Their success isn't just theirs. It belongs to every parent who will read this book and decide to believe that debt-free college is possible. It belongs to every student who applies for one more scholarship even after facing rejection. It belongs to every family who will choose faith over fear and strategy over surrender.

If Yahuah did it for my daughters, He can do it for yours too.

This journey is about more than money. It's about discipline, growth, and trust. When you combine faith with action, doors open in ways you couldn't have planned.

My prayer is that this book empowers you to move forward with confidence, patience, and belief. Yahuah has already gone before you. Your job is to take the next step.

As I close this book, my prayer is that every reader feels inspired to believe again, to prepare with purpose, and to trust Yahuah's timing in all things. Whether you're a parent, a student, or someone simply standing at the start of your own faith journey, know that it's never too late for Yahuah to write a new beginning in your story.

What began as a search for scholarships became a story of faith and restoration. Yahuah took my journey full circle, and I pray He does the same for you, turning every challenge into testimony and every prayer into purpose.

He is faithful. He is able. And He's waiting to do for you what He did for me. Trust Him. Obey Him. Walk forward in faith.

And watch Him turn your impossible into possible, your worry into worship, and your burden into blessing.

Your turn has come. Take the first step. Yahuah will meet you there.

***

# READER REFLECTION AND ACTION STEP

Take a quiet moment to reflect on your own journey.

What fears have been holding you back from starting?

What resources might already be around you that you haven't noticed yet?

Who are you called to stand in the gap for right now?

Write down one specific step you can take this week. Just one.

It might be searching for scholarships for thirty minutes.

It might be organizing documents into a single folder.

It might be having an honest conversation with your child about goals and finances.

It might simply be praying and asking Yahuah for clarity and direction.

Don't wait for the perfect plan.

Movement invites provision.

Preparation invites peace.

As you move forward, remember this.

You're not behind.

You're not unqualified.

You're not late.

You're right where you need to be to begin.

I told Monica this years ago, and I'm telling you the same thing now.

May Yahuah guide your steps, strengthen your resolve, and open doors that no one can close as you walk this journey in faith.

***

# A FINAL WORD OF ENCOURAGEMENT

You now have everything you need to begin. You have the knowledge, the strategies, the tools, and the timeline. Most importantly, you have the faith that Yahuah will provide.

Don't wait for perfect circumstances. Don't wait until you feel completely ready. Start now. Take one step. Then take another.

Yahuah has already gone before you. He has already opened doors you haven't seen yet. Your job is to walk through them with faith, consistency, and gratitude.

I'm praying for you and your family. I believe with you that debt-free college isn't just possible, it's your reality.

Now go. Begin. And watch Yahuah turn your faith into provision.

### From the Author's Voice:

*"This isn't the end of your journey. It's the beginning. Everything you need is already within reach. Trust Yahuah, do the work, and watch Him open doors that no one can close."*

***

# EPILOGUE: YOUR TURN - THE ACTION PLAN

This book began as a mother's determination to help her daughters attend college without the burden of student loans. It grew into a journey shaped by faith, effort, and obedience. Now, it's your turn.

When I think about where this journey began, I can still picture myself sitting at that kitchen table surrounded by papers, unsure of what to do next. I didn't know it then, but Yahuah was right there with me, guiding every step and every decision along the way.

He took a mother's worry and turned it into wisdom. He took my challenges and transformed them into strategies that would bless not only my family but many others. What started with uncertainty became a testimony of faith, persistence, and provision.

Watching Alayna and Laura succeed was more than a dream fulfilled, it was the manifestation of Yahuah's promises. The same hills and valleys that once tested my faith became proof of His goodness. Every scholarship, every opportunity, and every open door was evidence that Yahuah restores, provides, and multiplies beyond measure.

What brings me the greatest joy today is knowing that the story didn't end with my daughters. It continues through every student I've mentored and every family I've encouraged along the way. Each new success story adds another chapter to the legacy that Yahuah began in our home.

Looking back, I see how every prayer was answered, even the ones I didn't know how to pray. Every delay served a purpose, every "no" redirected us toward something better, and every blessing arrived at the perfect time.

The path from that anxious night at the kitchen table to today has been marked by Yahuah's faithfulness at every turn. He never left us. He never failed us. And He will not fail you either.

This action plan brings together everything I learned along the way. You don't need to do everything perfectly. You only need to begin.

## 1. Pray before you plan

Start every decision with prayer. Ask Yahuah for wisdom, clarity, and direction. Trust that He sees what you cannot and will guide your steps.

Prayer isn't just something you do once at the beginning. It should be woven throughout the entire process. Pray before searching for scholarships. Pray before writing essays. Pray before submitting applications. Pray when rejection letters arrive. Pray when award letters come. Let prayer be your anchor.

I prayed constantly during this journey. Some prayers were long and detailed. Others were short and desperate. All of them mattered. Yahuah heard **every one**, and He will hear yours too.

Make prayer a family practice. Pray with your child before they start working on applications. Pray together before submitting major scholarships. Let your child see that you're trusting Yahuah, not just relying on effort. That example will shape how they approach challenges for the rest of their lives.

## 2. Start early, but start anyway

If you can begin in ninth grade, do it. If you're starting senior year or later, don't let that stop you. The right time to begin is now.

Starting early gives you time to build skills, gather materials, and apply without pressure. But starting late doesn't disqualify you. I've seen students begin in the spring of their senior year and still secure significant funding. What matters most is that you start and that you stay consistent.

If your child is a freshman or sophomore, use this time to build their résumé. Get them involved in activities they care about. Encourage them to volunteer. Help them develop leadership skills. These experiences will become the foundation for their scholarship applications later.

If your child is a junior or senior, focus on what's available right now. Don't waste time regretting what you didn't do earlier. Start today and move forward with purpose.

## 3. Build your organization system

Create a system that works for you. Use a binder or digital folder, a tracking sheet, and a calendar to manage deadlines and requirements. Organization creates peace.

I can't stress this enough. Organization is the key to reducing stress and staying on top of deadlines. When everything has a place and you can see what needs to be done, the process becomes manageable.

Create sections in your binder for applications, essays, deadlines, recommendation letters, transcripts, and financial documents. Use dividers and sheet protectors to keep everything neat. Build a spreadsheet that tracks every scholarship you're pursuing, including the name, deadline, award amount, requirements, and status.

Color code your calendar. Red for urgent deadlines. Yellow for upcoming ones. Green for distant ones. Check your system daily. Update it regularly. Let it be your guide.

## 4. Search everywhere

Look beyond colleges. Search locally, online, through employers, churches, alumni groups, and community organizations. Scholarships are everywhere when you know where to look.

Don't limit yourself to the big national scholarships everyone knows about. Some of the best opportunities are local scholarships with less competition. Check with your employer. Visit your library. Read church bulletins. Attend community events. Talk to guidance counselors. Ask questions everywhere you go.

Use online databases like Fastweb, Scholarships.com, Bold.org, and Cappex. Set up profiles and check them daily. Sign up for email alerts. The more places you search, the more opportunities you'll find.

## 5. Be authentic in essays

Tell the truth about who you are and where you've been. Don't write what you think committees want to hear. Write from your heart. Authenticity stands out.

Scholarship committees read thousands of essays. What makes yours memorable isn't fancy vocabulary or perfect grammar. It's honesty. It's vulnerability. It's the willingness to share your real story, not a polished version of it.

Help your child identify their strengths, their challenges, their values, and their dreams. Encourage them to write about experiences that shaped them. Remind them that their story matters and that someone needs to hear it.

## 6. Apply consistently

Treat scholarships like a part-time job. Apply regularly, even when results are slow. Small awards add up, and persistence pays off. Consistency matters more than intensity. It's better to apply for two or three scholarships per week for several months than to apply for twenty in one weekend and then burn out.

Set aside dedicated time each week for scholarship work. Make it a routine. Stick to it. Even when you're tired. Even when results seem slow. Keep applying. The breakthrough is coming.

## 7. Handle rejection with faith

Every no isn't a failure. It's a redirect. Don't stop applying because of rejection. Keep moving forward and trust Yahuah's timing.

Rejection is part of the process. Every successful student has been rejected. What separates those who win from those who quit is the willingness to keep going after hearing no.

When rejection letters arrive, acknowledge the disappointment, but don't dwell on it. Pray. Regroup. Keep applying. Remember that every no brings you closer to the right yes.

Keep a folder of both rejections and acceptances. When discouragement comes, pull out the folder and look at what you've accomplished. Let the wins remind you that the process is working.

## 8. Understand financial aid and net cost

Don't assume sticker price is what you'll pay. Learn the difference between merit aid and need-based aid. Complete the FAFSA every year. Compare financial aid packages carefully. Know what's a grant (free money) versus a loan (borrowed money). Understanding these terms empowers you to make wise decisions.

The sticker price is just the starting point. After scholarships, grants, and aid are applied, the net price is what you actually pay. Two schools with the same sticker price can have very different net costs depending on the aid packages they offer.

Fill out the FAFSA even if you think you won't qualify for need-based aid. Many merit scholarships require it. Submit it as early as possible each year. Keep copies of all financial documents. Ask questions when you don't understand something. This is your money. You have a right to understand exactly where it's going.

## 9. Give thanks and celebrate every win

Celebrate completed applications, submitted essays, and every award received. Gratitude keeps your heart grounded and your faith strong.

Don't wait until the end to celebrate. Acknowledge progress along the way. Finishing an essay is worth celebrating. Submitting an application on time is worth celebrating. Every step forward matters.

When award letters arrive, celebrate with gratitude. Thank Yahuah. Thank the people who supported you. Let your child see that you recognize the blessings and that you don't take them for granted.

Gratitude isn't just good manners. It's a spiritual discipline. It keeps your heart humble and your perspective clear. It reminds you that every good gift comes from Yahuah.

These nine steps are your roadmap. But remember, you're not walking this path alone. Yahuah has already gone before you. He's already preparing the doors He's about to open. Your job is to take the first step and trust Him with the rest.

What began as my family's story can become yours too. The same faith that carried us will carry you. The same Yahuah who provided for my daughters will provide for yours.

Now it's your turn. Begin. And watch Him turn your faith into provision.

***

# APPENDIXES

## APPENDIX A

## MONTH-BY-MONTH SCHOLARSHIP TIMELINE

*A Four-Year Roadmap from Ninth Grade Through Senior Year*

The families who win the most scholarship money aren't the ones who work the hardest in senior year. They're the ones who started early and stayed consistent. This timeline will show you exactly what to do and when to do it, so you're never scrambling or guessing about your next steps.

### NINTH GRADE

### September - October: Foundation Building

This is the year to establish strong habits. Your child should focus on grades, getting involved in activities, and starting to think about their interests. Join at least one club or organization that aligns with their passions. Start a folder, digital or physical, where you save any scholarship information you come across, even if your child isn't eligible yet. Begin teaching your child how to track commitments and deadlines. These organizational skills will be essential later.

## November – December: Volunteer and Explore

Encourage your child to start volunteering. Scholarship committees love to see sustained community service over multiple years. Help your child identify one or two causes they care about and commit to serving regularly. This is also a good time to start exploring career interests. Have conversations about what fields interest them. Visit a career fair if your school offers one. The more clarity your child has early on, the easier it'll be to find targeted scholarships later.

## January – March: Academic Focus

Grades matter, especially freshman year. Many students assume they can recover from a rough ninth grade, but GPA is cumulative. Help your child develop good study habits now. If they're struggling in any subject, get help early. Tutoring, study groups, or extra time with teachers can make a huge difference. Keep encouraging involvement in extracurriculars. Consistency matters more than variety.

## April – June: Reflect and Plan Ahead

As the school year wraps up, sit down with your child and review what went well and what needs improvement. Did they keep up with their commitments? Did they maintain good grades? What activities do they want to continue next year? Use the summer to get ahead. If your child needs to improve test scores, consider summer SAT or ACT prep. If they want to add a new activity, summer's a great time to start.

## TENTH GRADE

### September - October: Building Momentum

Tenth grade is about deepening involvement. Your child should continue with the activities they started in ninth grade and begin taking on leadership roles when possible. This is also the time to start paying closer attention to academics. Encourage your child to take challenging courses that align with their intended major. Honors or AP classes can strengthen scholarship applications later. Begin researching scholarships casually. You're not applying yet, but you're learning what's out there and what requirements look like.

### November - December: Test Preparation Begins

If your child hasn't taken a practice SAT or ACT yet, now's the time. Many schools offer PSAT in tenth grade. Use the results to identify areas where your child needs improvement. Consider enrolling in a test prep course or using online resources. Strong test scores open doors to merit-based scholarships. Keep track of volunteer hours. Many scholarship applications ask for total hours served, so it helps to have an ongoing record.

### January - March: Expand and Explore

Encourage your child to explore new opportunities. Attend a leadership conference. Join a new club. Try out for a team. Apply for a summer program. Many competitive summer programs accept tenth graders, and participation in these programs can strengthen scholarship applications. If your child has a specific career interest, look for summer internships or shadowing opportunities. These experiences provide great material for future essays.

## April – June: Summer Planning

Plan a productive summer. Whether your child is working, volunteering, attending a program, or taking classes, make sure the summer is purposeful. Avoid long stretches of unstructured time. Scholarship committees want to see that students use their time wisely. If your child's old enough to work, encourage them to get a job. Work experience teaches responsibility and provides essay material. This is also a good time to start a résumé. Even if it's just one-page listing activities, volunteer work, and any leadership roles, having it started now makes it easier to update later.

## ELEVENTH GRADE

## September – October: Get Serious About Scholarships

Junior year is when the real work begins. This is the time to start actively searching for scholarships and building your application materials. Start by updating your child's résumé with everything they've done so far. List all activities, volunteer work, awards, leadership positions, and work experience. Create a list of teachers, coaches, and mentors who could write strong recommendation letters. These relationships take time to build, so start thinking about this now. Begin researching scholarships in earnest. Use databases like Fastweb, Scholarships.com, and Bold.org. Search for local scholarships through your school counselor, community organizations, and your employer. Start a tracking spreadsheet to organize deadlines and requirements.

## November – December: Request Recommendation Letters

November of junior year is an ideal time to ask teachers for recommendation letters. Teachers get flooded with requests in senior year, so asking early gives them time to write thoughtful letters. Choose teachers who know your child well and can speak to their character, work ethic, and growth. Provide them with a résumé and a brief summary of your child's goals. If your child's applying to summer programs or early scholarships, you may need letters sooner. Give teachers at least three to four weeks' notice. Take the SAT or ACT if your child hasn't already. Many students take it once in junior year and again in senior year to improve their scores. Some scholarships require minimum test scores, so having strong results opens up more opportunities.

## January – March: Peak Scholarship Season Begins

This is one of the busiest times for scholarships. Deadlines for local, regional, and national scholarships cluster in these months. Your child should be applying for two to three scholarships per week during this period. Focus on local scholarships first. These have less competition and higher success rates. Start writing essays now, even if your child isn't ready to submit them yet. Most scholarship essays ask similar questions, so you can often reuse or adapt them for multiple applications. Keep everything organized. Save every essay, every application, and every confirmation email. File the FAFSA as soon as possible after October 1st of senior year, but start gathering the necessary documents now. You'll need tax returns, W-2 forms, and bank statements. The earlier you file, the better your chances of receiving aid.

## April – June: Stay Consistent and Plan for Summer

Don't let up just because the school year's ending. Many scholarships have summer deadlines. Keep applying. Your child should also be finalizing their college list during this time. Visit campuses if possible. Attend information sessions. Start drafting college essays. The Common Application essay prompts are usually released in the spring, so your child can get a head start. Use the summer to apply for scholarships with fall deadlines. Work on essays. Gather documents. Prepare for senior year. This summer is critical. Stay productive.

## SENIOR YEAR

## July – August: Prepare and Organize

Senior year is the culmination of everything you've been working toward. Use the summer to get ahead. Finalize your child's résumé. Gather transcripts, test scores, and recommendation letters. If your child's applying through the Common Application, start filling out the basic information sections. Write or revise college essays. Many students wait until fall to do this, but summer's the perfect time. Complete scholarship applications with early fall deadlines. Organize your tracking system. Make sure you have a clear calendar of every deadline for the entire year.

## September – October: Launch Applications

College applications open, and so do many scholarship applications. Your child should submit early applications to colleges by early November if they're applying early decision or early action. FAFSA opens October 1st. File it as soon as possible. Many schools and states award aid on a first-come, first-served basis, so early filing matters. The CSS Profile (College Scholarship Service Profile) also opens in October. If any of your child's schools require it, submit it early. Continue applying for scholarships. Aim for two to three per week. Focus on scholarships with October and November deadlines.

## November – December: Stay on Track

This is a critical period. Make sure all college applications are submitted by their deadlines. Early decision and early action deadlines are usually in early November. Regular decision deadlines are typically in January. Double-check that transcripts, test scores, and recommendation letters have been sent to every school. Keep applying for scholarships. Many local scholarships open in late fall and early winter, so stay alert. If your child receives any scholarships or awards, report them to the financial aid office at the colleges they're considering. This helps with financial planning.

## January – March: Peak Scholarship Season for Seniors

This is the busiest scholarship season of the year. Deadlines for local, regional, and national scholarships are everywhere. Your child should be applying aggressively during this time. Prioritize local scholarships. These often have deadlines in

February and March and are less competitive than national programs. Many high schools host scholarship nights or workshops in January and February. Attend these. Counselors often share information about local opportunities that aren't widely advertised. If your child's been accepted to colleges, compare financial aid packages carefully. Look at the net price, not just the sticker price. Consider appealing for more aid if necessary.

## April – May: Decision Time

By late March or early April, your child should have heard from most colleges. Financial aid packages should also be finalized. Now's the time to compare offers and make a final decision. National College Decision Day is May 1st. Your child must commit to one school by this date and submit a deposit. Keep applying for scholarships, even after committing to a school. Many scholarships for incoming freshmen have deadlines in late spring. Once your child's chosen a school, report all scholarships to the financial aid office. Some schools allow you to stack outside scholarships. Others may reduce institutional aid if you bring in too much outside funding. Understand the policy so there aren't any surprises.

## June – August: Prepare for College

Scholarship work doesn't end when senior year ends. Continue searching for scholarships for current college students. Many organizations offer awards specifically for students already enrolled in college. Make sure all scholarship funds have been sent to your child's school.

Follow up with scholarship organizations if payments are delayed. Organize all documents related to scholarships and financial aid. You'll need this information for tax purposes and for future aid applications. Celebrate. Your child worked hard. You worked hard. Take time to acknowledge what you accomplished together.

## ONGOING THROUGHOUT ALL FOUR YEARS

*Track Volunteer Hours*

Keep a running log of all volunteer work. Note the organization, dates, and total hours. Many scholarship applications ask for this information, and it's hard to remember details later.

*Save Awards and Recognitions*

Any time your child receives an award, certificate, or recognition, save it. These can be listed on scholarship applications and résumés.

*Build Relationships with Teachers and Mentors*

Strong recommendation letters come from people who know your child well. Encourage your child to build genuine relationships with teachers, coaches, and mentors throughout high school.

*Update the Résumé Regularly*

Every time your child takes on a new role, joins a new activity, or earns a new honor, add it to the résumé immediately. Updating it as you go is much easier than trying to remember everything later.

*Stay Organized*

Keep a master folder with copies of every application, essay, transcript, test score, and award letter. Organization saves time and reduces stress.

*Pray and Trust the Process*

This journey requires faith. Pray before every application. Pray through every rejection. Pray in gratitude for every win. Yahuah's timing is perfect, and His provision is sure.

*Final Thoughts on Timing*

This timeline may look overwhelming at first, but remember that you don't have to do everything at once. The key is to start early and stay consistent. A little progress each month adds up to major results over four years.

If you're starting late, don't panic. Begin wherever you are and move forward with focus and determination. It's never too late to start, but the sooner you begin, the more opportunities you'll have.

Follow this timeline, adjust it to fit your family's needs, and trust that Yahuah will guide every step. You're not alone in this process.

### From the Author's Voice:

*"Time is your greatest asset in the scholarship process. The earlier you start; the more opportunities you create. But even if you're starting late, remember that focused effort in a short time can still produce powerful results."*

***

# APPENDIX B

# RESOURCE SECTION: TEMPLATES AND TOOLS

## Scholarship Tracking Spreadsheet Template

Create a spreadsheet with the following columns:

_Scholarship Name_

_Organization_

_Deadline_

_Award Amount_

_Requirements_

_Status_

_Date Submitted_

_Notes_

## How to use:

- Add every scholarship you find, even if you're not sure you'll apply.

- Update the Status column regularly (Not Started, In Progress, Submitted, Awarded, Rejected).

- Use color coding: Red for urgent deadlines, Yellow for upcoming, Green for completed.

- Review this spreadsheet weekly during your dedicated scholarship time.

## Monthly Scholarship Calendar Template

*September - November (Junior/Senior Year)*

- Week 1: Research and list 10 new scholarships.
- Week 2: Gather materials (transcripts, letters, essays).
- Week 3: Complete and submit 2-3 applications.
- Week 4: Follow up on submitted applications, search for new opportunities.

*December - February*

- Focus on scholarships with January-March deadlines.
- Update résumé and activities list.
- Request new recommendation letters if needed.
- Apply for local and community scholarships.

*March - May*

- Priority: Scholarships with April-June deadlines.
- Apply for summer program scholarships.
- Complete FAFSA renewal (if applicable).
- Finalize college choice based on financial aid packages.

*June - August*

- Search for scholarships for current college students.
- Apply for departmental and major-specific scholarships.
- Look for last-minute opportunities.
- Organize documents for fall semester.

## Scholarship Binder Organization System

*Section 1: Personal Documents*

- Official transcripts (keep 5-10 copies).

- Résumé/Activities list.

- Test scores (SAT/ACT).

- Letters of recommendation (organized by recommender).

- Personal statement/essays (master copies).

*Section 2: Scholarship Opportunities*

- Local scholarships.

- State scholarships.

- National scholarships.

- Major-specific scholarships.

- Organization by deadline date.

*Section 3: Completed Applications*

- Copies of submitted applications.

- Confirmation emails.

- Award letters received.

- Rejection letters (for tracking purposes).

*Section 4: Financial Information*

- FAFSA confirmation.

- CSS Profile (if applicable) (College Scholarship Service Profile).

- Financial aid award letters from colleges.

- Scholarship disbursement information.

*Section 5: Calendar and Checklist*

- Monthly calendar with deadlines.

- Master checklist of all applications.

- Contact information for scholarship coordinators.

## Essay Prompt Response Template

## Step 1: Understand the Prompt Write the prompt in your own words:

_______________________________________

_______________________________________

_______________________________________

_______________________________________

Key words in the prompt:

_______________________________________

_______________________________________

_______________________________________

_______________________________________

What is the scholarship committee really asking?

_______________________________________

_______________________________________

_______________________________________

_______________________________________

## Step 2: Brainstorm List 3-5 experiences that relate to this prompt:

1.________________________________________________

2.________________________________________________

3.________________________________________________

4.________________________________________________

5.________________________________________________


## Step 3: Choose Your Story Which experience best demonstrates:

________________________________________________

________________________________________________

________________________________________________

________________________________________________


## Step 4: Outline Introduction (Hook):

________________________________________________

________________________________________________

________________________________________________

________________________________________________

## Conclusion (Tie back to prompt):

________________________________________________

________________________________________________

________________________________________________

________________________________________________

## Step 5: Write and Revise

- First draft: Write freely without editing.

- Second draft: Focus on clarity and flow.

- Third draft: Proofread for grammar and spelling.

- Final review: Read aloud to check for authenticity.

## Recommendation Letter Request Template

## Email to Potential Recommender:

Subject: Recommendation Letter Request for [Scholarship Name]

Dear [Teacher/Mentor Name],

I hope this email finds you well. I'm applying for [scholarship name], which [briefly describes scholarship and why it matters to you]. The deadline is [date].

I would be honored if you would write a letter of recommendation on my behalf. I believe you can speak to [specific qualities: my leadership abilities, my work ethic, my growth in your class, etc.].

To make this easier for you, I have attached:

- My current résumé.

- A list of my accomplishments and activities.

- Information about the scholarship and what they're looking for.

- The submission instructions and deadline.

The letter is due by [date]. If this timeline works for you, please let me know, and I will provide any additional information you need.

Thank you for considering this request. Your guidance has meant so much to me, and I'm grateful for your support.

Sincerely, [Your Name]

## What to Include in Your Packet:

- Résumé with academic achievements, extracurricular activities, and community service.

- Brief personal statement about your goals.

- Specific points you hope they will address (optional, but helpful).

- Addressed and stamped envelope (if mailing) or submission link.

- Deadline reminder.

- Thank you note template they can use.

## Weekly Scholarship Search Routine

*Monday: Local Search (30 minutes)*

- Check the school counseling office website.

- Review local newspaper and community bulletins.

- Visit the library for local scholarship books.

- Check with local organizations (Rotary, Kiwanis, Lions Club).

*Tuesday: Online Database Search (45 minutes)*

- Check Fastweb for new matches.

- Search Scholarships.com.

- Review Bold.org opportunities.

- Check Cappex updates.

*Wednesday: Organization-Specific Search (30 minutes)*

- Research scholarships related to your intended major.

- Check professional associations in your field.

- Look for scholarships related to hobbies/interests.

- Search faith-based scholarship opportunities.

*Thursday: Employer and Alumni Search (30 minutes)*

- Check parent/guardian employer benefits.

- Research college alumni association scholarships.

- Look for scholarships from parents' professional organizations.

- Search for dependent scholarships.

*Friday: Application Work (1-2 hours)*

- Write or revise essays.

- Complete application forms.

- Gather required documents.

- Submit completed applications.

*Saturday/Sunday: Review and Plan (30 minutes)*

- Update tracking spreadsheet.

- Review upcoming deadlines.

- Plan next week's priorities.

- Celebrate completed submissions.

## Sample Essay: Overcoming Challenges

Note: *This is a composite example based on successful essays. Use it as a guide for structure and authenticity, not to copy.*

## Prompt: Describe a challenge you have faced and how you overcame it.

The smell of disinfectant still makes me think of my grandmother. For two years, I spent every Saturday morning at Sunrise Assisted Living, not as a volunteer fulfilling service hours, but as a granddaughter determined to be present during my grandmother's final chapter.

When my grandmother was diagnosed with Alzheimer's, my family faced a choice. Place her in a facility and visit occasionally, or stay involved in her daily care. We chose presence. My parents handled weekday visits, and I took Saturdays.

At first, the visits were painful. My grandmother, who once recited poetry from memory and solved crossword puzzles in ink, now struggled to remember my name. Some days she thought I was her sister. Other days she didn't recognize me at all. I would leave in tears, wondering if my presence even mattered.

But I kept showing up. I learned to meet her where she was instead of mourning who she used to be. I brought photo albums and let her tell me stories, even when the details changed each time. I played the hymns she loved and watched her face light up with recognition. I sat in comfortable silence when words failed us both.

Through this experience, I learned that love isn't diminished by the loss of memory. I learned that showing up matters, even when it's hard. I learned that some of life's most important work happens in quiet moments no one else sees.

This challenge taught me resilience, compassion, and the value of faithful presence. These are the qualities I will carry into my nursing career, where I hope to care for patients and families navigating their own difficult journeys.

My grandmother passed away last spring. At her funeral, the staff from Sunrise told my family that my weekly visits had brought her more joy than we realized. That confirmation reminded me that faithfulness is never wasted, even when we can't see its full impact.

(*Word count: 345*)

## Why This Essay Works:

- Opens with a sensory detail that draws readers in.

- Tells a specific story, not vague generalities.

- Shows vulnerability and growth.

- Connects the experience to future goals.

- Ends with reflection and meaning.

- Stays authentic to the student's voice.

## Scholarship Application Checklist

*Before You Apply:*

☐ Read the entire application carefully.

☐ Check eligibility requirements (GPA, location, major, etc.).

☐ Note the deadline and add it to your calendar.

☐ Understand what materials are required.

☐ Save the application to your scholarship folder.

*Gathering Materials:*

☐ Request transcript (allow 1-2 weeks).

☐ Request recommendation letters (allow 2-4 weeks).

☐ Prepare résumé/activities list.

☐ Write or adapt essay to fit prompt.

☐ Collect any special requirements (portfolio, video, etc.).

*Application Review:*

☐ Proofread all written materials.

☐ Check that essay answers the prompt.

☐ Verify all required documents are included.

☐ Confirm contact information is correct.

☐ Make sure essay is within word count.

☐ Have someone else review your application.

*Submission:*

☐ Submit before the deadline (aim for 2-3 days early).

☐ Save confirmation email or screenshot.

☐ Update tracking spreadsheet.

☐ Add to "Submitted" section of binder.

☐ Set reminder to follow up in 4-6 weeks if no response.

*After Submission:*

☐ Send thank-you notes to recommenders.

☐ Keep copies of everything submitted.

☐ Watch for communication from scholarship organization.

☐ Respond promptly to any requests for additional information.

☐ If awarded, send thank-you letter to donors.

☐ If rejected, stay encouraged and keep applying.

## Financial Aid Comparison Worksheet

*Use this worksheet to compare financial aid packages from different schools:*

---

---

---

---

Cost of Attendance:

---

---

---

---

Financial Aid Offered:

Grants (doesn't need to be repaid):

Scholarships (doesn't need to be repaid):

Work-Study (earned through employment):

Federal Student Loans (must be repaid):

Parent PLUS Loans (must be repaid):

Private Loans (must be repaid):

Net Cost: Total Cost minus Grants/Scholarships =

---

---

---

---

Loan Burden: Total loans needed per year =

_______________________________________________

_______________________________________________

_______________________________________________

_______________________________________________

## Renewal Requirements:

Minimum GPA to keep scholarships:

_______________________________________________

_______________________________________________

_______________________________________________

_______________________________________________

## Notes:

_______________________________________________

_______________________________________________

_______________________________________________

_______________________________________________

Repeat this worksheet for each school and compare the net costs and loan burdens to make an informed decision.

***

# FREQUENTLY ASKED QUESTIONS

## 1. When should we start looking for scholarships?

The best time to start is in ninth grade, but it's never too late. Starting early allows you to build a strong résumé, develop relationships with teachers who can write recommendation letters, and spread out the application work over several years. However, I've worked with families who started in the spring of senior year and still secured significant funding. The key is to start now, wherever you are, and stay consistent.

## 2. What if my child's grades aren't perfect? Can they still get scholarships?

Yes. While some scholarships are GPA-based, many focus on other qualities like community service, leadership, character, perseverance, creativity, or field of study. I've seen students with average GPAs win thousands of dollars in scholarships because they had compelling stories, strong work ethics, or unique talents. Don't let grades stop you from applying. There are scholarships for every type of student.

## 3. How can we stay motivated when the process feels overwhelming?

Remember why you started. College is an investment in your child's future, and scholarships make that investment possible without the burden of debt. Celebrate small wins along the way. Keep a folder of acceptance letters and completed applications to remind yourself of progress. Pray regularly and trust that Yahuah is guiding the process. Lean on your support system, whether that is family, friends, or a mentor. And most importantly, take it one step at a time. You do not have to do everything at once. Consistency over time will get you to the finish line.

## 4. What advice would you give to a parent starting this journey today?

Start now. Do not wait for the perfect time or the perfect plan. Begin with prayer, build an organization system, and take it one step at a time. Trust that Yahuah will provide, but do your part by staying consistent and committed. Celebrate progress, not just outcomes. And remember, this journey is not just about money. It is about teaching your child discipline, resilience, and faith. The scholarships are the reward, but the process is what shapes character. You can do this. Yahuah has already gone before you. Take the first step, and He will meet you there.

## 5. Can my child stack scholarships, or will one cancel out another?

In most cases, yes, you can stack scholarships. However, some colleges have policies that limit the total amount of outside scholarships a student can receive, especially if the combined total exceeds the cost of attendance. Check with the financial aid office at each school your child is considering to understand their stacking policies. Many schools allow students to keep scholarships up to the full cost of attendance, and some even allow students to use excess scholarship funds for things like laptops or study abroad programs.

## 6. Are online scholarship databases safe? How do we avoid scams?

Legitimate scholarship databases like Fastweb, Scholarships.com, Bold.org, and Cappex are safe and free to use. Never pay to apply for a scholarship. If a scholarship asks for an application fee, it's likely a scam. Be cautious of scholarships that guarantee awards or ask for banking information upfront. Stick to well-known databases, scholarships from reputable organizations, and opportunities recommended by your school counselor.

## 7. How do we choose which scholarships to apply for?

Start by reading the eligibility requirements carefully. If your child doesn't meet the basic criteria (GPA, location, major, demographic), move on. Focus on scholarships where your child is a strong match. Prioritize local scholarships, employer-based scholarships, and awards that align with your child's interests, background, or career goals. Those tend to have less competition and higher success rates.

## 8. Can parents help with the scholarship process, or should students do it alone?

Parents should absolutely help. High school students are learning how to manage complex tasks, and the scholarship process can be overwhelming. Your role is to guide, organize, and hold your child accountable. Help them build their tracking system, review their essays, and manage deadlines. However, make sure your child is doing the actual writing and submitting. Scholarship committees can tell when a parent wrote the essay instead of the student.

## 9. What if my child doesn't know what to write about in their essays?

Start by asking questions. What challenges have they overcome? What experiences shaped who they are? What are they passionate about? What do they want to do with their education? The best essays come from honest reflection, not from trying to impress a committee. Encourage your child to write about real experiences, even if they seem small or ordinary. Authenticity always stands out.

## 10. How do we handle scholarship money that exceeds the cost of attendance?

If your child receives more scholarship money than the cost of tuition, fees, room, and board, the excess funds are typically refunded to the student. These funds can be used for other education-related expenses like books, a laptop, transportation, or living expenses. Some students use excess scholarship funds to study abroad or participate in unpaid internships. When Alayna and Laura had pending refunds, I would contact the financial aid office and ask them to roll the refund over to the next semester because we did not know if we would come up short later. You should check with your school to see if they allow refunds to be rolled over. Also check with the financial aid office and the IRS so you understand any tax implications of excess scholarship funds.

## 11. Do we need to report scholarships to the college?

Yes. Most colleges require students to report outside scholarships to the financial aid office. This is important because scholarships can affect need-based aid packages. However, in most cases, outside scholarships reduce loans or work-study first before affecting grants. Always communicate with the financial aid office to understand how scholarships will impact your overall package.

## 12. Can my child apply for scholarships after they start college?

Yes. Many scholarships are available to current college students, including departmental scholarships, major-specific awards, and scholarships for upperclassmen. Encourage your child to continue searching and applying throughout their college years. Some of the best scholarships are only available to students who have already completed a year or two of college and can demonstrate academic success at the university level.

## 13. How can we stay motivated when the process feels overwhelming?

Remember why you started. College is an investment in your child's future, and scholarships make that investment possible without the burden of debt. Celebrate small wins along the way. Keep a folder of acceptance letters and completed applications to remind yourself of progress. Pray regularly and trust that Yahuah is guiding the process. Lean on your support system, whether that's family, friends, or a mentor. And most importantly, take it one step at a time. You don't have to do everything at once. Consistency over time will get you to the finish line.

## 14. What role does faith play in the scholarship process?

For our family, faith was the foundation of everything. We prayed before every decision, trusted Yahuah's timing through delays and rejections, and celebrated every win as evidence of His provision. Faith doesn't replace effort, but it sustains you when the process gets hard. It reminds you that you're not in this alone and that Yahuah sees what you cannot see. Prayer, gratitude, and trust in His plan will carry you further than stress and anxiety ever could.

## 15. What is the biggest mistake families make during the scholarship process?

The biggest mistake is giving up too soon. Many families apply for a handful of scholarships, face a few rejections, and quit. They assume scholarships are too competitive or that their child isn't qualified. The truth is, persistence is the key. The families who succeed are the ones who keep applying even after rejection, who stay organized, and who treat scholarships like a long-term commitment, not a one-time effort.

***

# APPENDIX D

## COMMON MISTAKES TO AVOID

*Learning from Others So You Don't Have to Learn the Hard Way.*

Over the years of helping families navigate the scholarship process, I have seen the same mistakes repeated again and again. Some mistakes cost families a few hundred dollars. Others cost them tens of thousands.

The good news is that every single one of these mistakes is avoidable. You just have to know what to watch for.

I share these not to discourage you, but to prepare you. If you can avoid even one of these mistakes, this section will have been worth reading.

### Mistake 1: Expecting Your Child to Do This Alone

This is the biggest mistake I see, and it happens more often than you might think. Parents assume that because their child is old enough to drive or vote, they should be able to handle the scholarship process independently. That assumption costs families thousands of dollars every year.

The scholarship process is complex. It requires organization, time management, attention to detail, and the ability to juggle multiple deadlines while keeping up with schoolwork, extracurricular, and everything else teenagers are managing. Even the most responsible student needs guidance and accountability.

I've worked with families where the parent handed the responsibility entirely to the child and then wondered why nothing got done. The student meant well. They had good intentions. But without a system, without regular check-ins, and without someone holding them accountable, applications sat unfinished. Deadlines passed. Opportunities disappeared.

Your role as a parent isn't to do the work for your child. Your role is to guide, support, organize, and follow up. You're the project manager. Your child is the content creator. Both roles matter. When parents tell me, "I'm letting my child handle it because they need to learn responsibility," I understand the intention. But the scholarship process isn't the time to teach responsibility through trial and error. The stakes are too high. You can teach responsibility by involving them in the process while also making sure things actually get done.

Check in regularly. Ask to see drafts. Review deadlines together. Make sure your child knows you're invested and paying attention. That accountability makes all the difference.

## Mistake 2: Not Following Up on Assignments

This mistake goes hand in hand with the first one. Parents assign tasks to their child, such as finishing an essay or requesting a recommendation letter, but then they never follow up to make sure it happens.

I worked with one family where the mother asked her son to request letters of recommendation from two teachers in

October. She assumed he had done it. In January, when we were preparing to submit applications, we discovered he never asked. The teachers were now overwhelmed with requests from other students, and it was too late to get thoughtful, detailed letters.

That oversight cost him scholarships. Several applications required two letters of recommendation, and because he did not have them, he could not apply.

Following up isn't nagging. Following up is good parenting. Set deadlines. Check progress. If your child says they finished something, ask to see it. If they say they sent something, ask for confirmation. I recommend weekly check-ins during scholarship season. Sit down together every Sunday evening and review what needs to be done that week. Mark completed tasks. Adjust priorities. Celebrate progress. Those fifteen-minute conversations keep everything on track.

## Mistake 3: Giving False Hope and Expecting to Win Every Scholarship

Some parents approach scholarships with unrealistic expectations. They think that if their child applies for ten scholarships, they should win ten scholarships. When the rejections start coming, they get discouraged and quit.

I have to be honest with families from the beginning. You're going to face rejection. A lot of rejection. Even the best students with perfect GPAs and impressive resumes get rejected far more often than they get accepted.

Scholarship committees receive hundreds or thousands of applications. They can only choose a few winners. That means most applicants won't win, no matter how qualified they are. Rejection isn't a reflection of your child's worth or potential. It's simply the reality of a competitive process.

If you go into this process expecting to win every scholarship you apply for, you will be devastated by the outcomes. But if you go in understanding that you might apply for fifty scholarships and win five, you will have the right mindset. Those five wins could still add up to ten or twenty thousand dollars.

I tell parents to celebrate effort, not just outcomes. Celebrate the fact that your child finished an application. Celebrate that they met a deadline. Celebrate that they're trying. The wins will come, but they will come through persistence, not perfection.

## Mistake 4: Waiting Until Senior Year

This is the mistake that costs families the most money, and it's the one I see most often. The sad truth is that the majority of families I work with wait until senior year to start looking for scholarships. By then, they have already missed hundreds of opportunities.

When parents come to me in the fall of senior year expecting me to perform a miracle, I do my best to help, but I can't undo the lost time. We can still find scholarships and we can still make progress, but we are starting from behind.

I had one parent who was very upset with me because her child had to delay college for a year due to poor planning.

She waited until the spring of senior year to reach out for help. By that time, most major deadlines had passed. Her daughter did not have enough funding to start in the fall, so she had to take a gap year and reapply the following cycle.

That delay was not because her daughter was not qualified. It was not because scholarships were not available. It was simply because they started too late.

If you're reading this and your child is in ninth, tenth, or eleventh grade, you're ahead of most families. Use that time wisely. Start researching now. Start building your system now. Start applying as soon as your child becomes eligible.

If you're reading this and your child is already a senior, don't panic. It isn't too late. But you need to move quickly and stay focused. Every day matters.

## Mistake 5: Not Proofreading Applications and Essays

This mistake seems small, but it has big consequences. I've seen students lose scholarships because of spelling errors, grammatical mistakes, or incomplete sentences in their essays.

Scholarship committees read hundreds of essays. When they see careless errors, it sends a message that the student did not take the application seriously. Why would they award money to someone who couldn't be bothered to proofread?

I also see parents who don't read what their child wrote before it gets submitted. They trust that their child did a good job, and they don't want to be overbearing. But reading your child's essay isn't about control. It's about quality assurance.

You don't have to rewrite their essay. You don't have to change their voice. But you should absolutely read it and check for errors. Look for typos. Look for unclear sentences. Look for places where the essay does not answer the prompt.

I recommend having at least two people review every essay before it's submitted. The student should read it out loud to catch awkward phrasing. A parent should read it for errors and clarity. If possible, a teacher or counselor should also review it. The more eyes on an essay, the better it will be.

One more thing. Read the application instructions carefully. I've seen students submit essays that did not follow the word count limit or did not address the actual question being asked. Those applications get disqualified immediately, no matter how good the writing is.

## Mistake 6: Skipping Scholarships That Seem Too Small or Too Specific

When I was helping my daughters apply for scholarships, I almost made this mistake myself. I would see a scholarship for five hundred dollars and think, "That isn't worth the time." Or I would see a scholarship that seemed like it did not perfectly match their field of study, and I would skip it.

I am glad I did not follow that instinct. Some of the scholarships my daughters won were smaller awards that I almost ignored. But those small scholarships added up. Five hundred here. One thousand there. Before long, we had several thousand dollars just from the awards I almost skipped.

I also learned that even if a scholarship isn't specifically for your child's major, it might still be worth applying. Many scholarships have broad eligibility. As long as your child meets the basic requirements, apply. Don't disqualify yourself before the committee has a chance to consider you.

The only exception is if the scholarship explicitly requires something your child doesn't have. If it says "must be majoring in nursing" and your child is majoring in engineering, then skip it. But if it says "preference given to STEM majors" and your child is in business, still apply. You never know.

## Mistake 7: Not Keeping Copies of Everything

I can't tell you how many times I've worked with students who submitted an application and then couldn't remember what they wrote. When they need to reference that essay for another application or when a scholarship committee asks for clarification, they have nothing to refer back to.

Keep copies of everything. Every essay. Every application. Every confirmation email. Every award letter. Create a digital folder and save it all.

This habit also protects you if something goes wrong. I had one student who submitted an application through an online portal, but the system glitched and the application was never received. Because she had saved a copy, she was able to resubmit quickly and still meet the deadline. Keeping records also helps when it's time to report scholarships to your college's financial aid office. You will need documentation of every award. If you have been saving everything along the way, that process is simple.

## Mistake 8: Giving Up After a Few Rejections

I mentioned this earlier, but it's worth repeating. The families who succeed in the scholarship process aren't the ones who never face rejection. They're the ones who keep going despite rejection.

I've seen students apply for thirty scholarships and hear nothing but silence or rejections. Then on application thirty-one, they win five thousand dollars. If they had quit at application thirty, they would have walked away with nothing.

Rejection doesn't mean you're doing something wrong. It means you're playing the game. Every no brings you closer to a yes. Every rejection teaches you something that will make your next application stronger.

If you find yourself getting discouraged, go back and read your child's essays. Remind yourself why they deserve these opportunities. Look at the awards you have already received, even if they're small. Celebrate progress. And then get back to work.

The families who win aren't the smartest or the most talented. They're the most persistent.

## Final Thoughts on Mistakes

Every family I've worked with, including my own, has made at least one of these mistakes. That's normal. The key is to recognize the mistake, adjust, and keep moving forward.

If you're reading this list and realizing you have already made some of these mistakes, don't panic. It isn't too late to course correct. Start following up more consistently. Start proofreading more carefully. Start applying to scholarships you previously overlooked. The fact that you're reading this book means you're already ahead of most families. You're learning. You're preparing. You're taking this seriously.

Avoid these mistakes, stay consistent, and trust the process. The scholarships will come.

### *From the Author's Voice*

*"Mistakes are expensive teachers, but learning from someone else's mistakes is free. Take the lessons, skip the consequences, and keep moving forward."*

***

# APPENDIX E

## SOURCES AND FURTHER READING

The research, statistics, and resources referenced throughout this book come from trusted organizations dedicated to helping families navigate college affordability. I have also included scholarship databases, financial aid resources, and contact information so you can continue your journey with confidence.

### RESEARCH SOURCES CITED IN THIS BOOK

*College Board*

The College Board provides annual reports on college costs, financial aid trends, and student debt statistics. Their "Trends in College Pricing" publication was referenced in Chapter 1 for average annual costs of public and private universities.
Website: collegeboard.org

*National Scholarship Providers Association (NSPA)*

The NSPA is the leading organization for scholarship providers. Their research on unclaimed scholarships, referenced in Chapter 7, helped correct common myths about billions in unused scholarship funds.
Website: scholarshipproviders.org

*Sallie Mae -- "How America Pays for College"*

This annual report, cited in Chapter 8, provides data on how families fund higher education, including average

scholarship awards and the percentage of students receiving aid.
Website: salliemae.com

*Bureau of Labor Statistics (BLS)*

The BLS offers comprehensive employment and salary data by occupation and industry. This resource, referenced in Chapter 9, helped illustrate career outcomes and starting salaries for different majors.
Website: bls.gov

*Federal Student Aid (U.S. Department of Education)*

Federal Student Aid provides official information about FAFSA, Pell Grants, student loans, and the total cost of attendance. Data on unclaimed Pell Grants and financial aid definitions in Chapter 6 came from this source. .
Website: studentaid.gov

*The Gates Scholarship*

One of the most competitive and prestigious scholarships in the country. Acceptance rate statistics referenced in Chapter 5 came from their publicly available program data.
Website: thegatesscholarship.org

*Coca-Cola Scholars Program*

Another highly competitive national scholarship program. Selection rate data cited in Chapter 5 demonstrates the competitive nature of large national scholarships.
Website: coca-colascholars.org

*Scholarship America*

A leading scholarship and education support organization that administers employer-sponsored scholarship programs. Referenced in Chapter 3 for workplace tuition assistance programs.
Website: scholarshipamerica.org

*Georgetown University Center on Education and the Workforce*

Provides research on the economic value of education and career pathways. While not directly cited, their work informed discussions on return on investment for different degree programs.
Website: cew.georgetown.edu

## RECOMMENDED SCHOLARSHIP DATABASES

These are free, legitimate scholarship search platforms. I used all of them during my daughters' scholarship journey, and I recommend them to every family I work with.

*Fastweb*

One of the largest and most established scholarship databases. Create a profile, and the site will match your child with scholarships based on their interests, background, and qualifications.
Website: fastweb.com

*Scholarships.com*

Another comprehensive database with thousands of scholarships. The site is easy to navigate and allows students to filter by deadline, award amount, and eligibility.

Website: scholarships.com

*Bold.org*

A newer platform with a user-friendly interface. Bold.org features scholarships with unique essay prompts and lower competition than some national programs.
Website: bold.org

*Cappex*

Combines scholarship searching with college matching. Students can explore schools and scholarships in one place.
Website: cappex.com

*Niche*

Offers scholarships, college reviews, and rankings. Known for easy-to-enter monthly scholarships, though competition can be high.
Website: niche.com

*College-Specific Scholarships*

Always check the financial aid pages of colleges your child is interested in. Many schools offer merit scholarships, departmental awards, and honors program funding directly through their websites.

*Local Resources*

Do not overlook local opportunities. Check with your high school guidance counselor, community foundation, church, employer, civic organizations (Rotary, Kiwanis, Lions Club), and local businesses. These scholarships often have the least competition and the highest success rates.

## FINANCIAL AID RESOURCES

*FAFSA (Free Application for Federal Student Aid)*

Required for federal financial aid, including grants, work-study, and loans. File as early as possible after October 1st of your child's senior year. Many states and schools award aid on a first-come, first-served basis.
Website: fafsa.gov

*CSS Profile (College Scholarship Service Profile)*

Used by some private colleges to award institutional aid. Check each school's financial aid page to see if they require the CSS Profile in addition to FAFSA.
Website: cssprofile.collegeboard.org

*Federal Student Aid Information Center*

For questions about FAFSA, federal loans, or aid eligibility, contact the Federal Student Aid Information Center.
Phone: 1-800-433-3243

*Net Price Calculators*

Every college is required to have a net price calculator on its website. Use these tools to estimate what your family will actually pay after scholarships and grants are applied.

*State-Based Financial Aid Programs*

Many states offer grants and scholarships to residents attending in-state schools. Search for "[Your State] higher education financial aid" to find your state's resources.

***

# BOOKS FOR FURTHER READING

While this book provides a comprehensive roadmap, there are other helpful resources for families navigating college planning and financial aid.

*"Paying for College Without Going Broke" by The Princeton Review*

A detailed guide to financial aid, merit scholarships, and strategies for reducing college costs.

*"The Financial Aid Handbook" by Carol Stack and Ruth Vedvik*

Offers practical advice on filling out the FAFSA, appealing financial aid decisions, and understanding award letters.

*"Debt-Free U: How I Paid for an Outstanding College Education Without Loans, Scholarships, or Mooching off My Parents" by Zac Bissonnette*

A student's perspective on attending college affordably through strategic school choice and smart financial planning.

*"How to Go to College Almost for Free" by Ben Kaplan*

Written by a student who won over $90,000 in scholarships, this book shares strategies for finding and winning awards.

***

# ABOUT THE AUTHOR

*Abbie P. Huckleby* is the founder of Parent Project LLC, a scholarship preparation program dedicated to helping families fund higher education through faith, organization, and proven strategy. After guiding her own two daughters to graduate from college debt-free, Abbie made it her mission to share that knowledge with others. She now mentors families nationwide, helping students unlock scholarship opportunities while strengthening their confidence and faith. Through Parent Project LLC, Abbie continues to lead workshops, community presentations, speaking engagements, and one-on-one consultations that have helped countless families secure scholarships and financial freedom.

## Connect with the Author

Thank you for reading *Faith, Favor, and Funding*. My hope is that this book inspired you to believe in what's possible, to prepare with purpose, and to trust Yahuah's timing in every step of your family's journey.

I would love to hear your story, celebrate your wins, and help you take the next step toward your student's success.

✉ Email: abbie@parentprojectllc.com

📞 Phone: 832-600-5413

🔗 LinkedIn: linkedin.com/in/abbie-huckleby

📷 Instagram: instagram.com/parentprojectscholarships

👥 Facebook: facebook.com/ParentProject

🎵 TikTok: tiktok.com/@parentprojectllc

🌐 Website: Visit www.parentprojectllc.com for more resources and scholarship tools.

📢 Speaking Engagements: Abbie is available for workshops, church events, conferences, and community presentations. Contact her to bring scholarship strategy and faith-based guidance to your organization.

Scan the QR Code Below to Book a Consultation

***